SSI Monograph

CIVIL-MILITARY RELATIONS IN MEDVEDEV'S RUSSIA

Stephen J. Blank
Editor

January 2011

*****

Published by Books Express Publishing
Books Express, 2011
ISBN 978-1-780395-52-4

Books Express publications are available from all good retail and online booksellers. For
publishing proposals and direct ordering please contact us at: info@books-express.com

CONTENTS

FOREWORD

The papers collected here represent the Strategic Studies Institute's (SSI) continuing activity to foster dialogue on topical issues in international security among experts from the United States and abroad. These papers are taken from the conference that SSI conducted on January 25-26, 2010, entitled, "Contemporary Issues in International Security," at the Finnish embassy in Washington, DC. This was the second conference that SSI organized, bringing together U.S., Russian, and European experts to discuss important questions in contemporary world affairs.

We hope to continue these conferences on an annual basis because of the importance of such dialogue among experts and governments. But rather than publishing the papers as a book, which we did in 2009, SSI has decided to publish them on a panel-by-panel basis. This particular collection is devoted to the question of civil-military relations in Russia, a topic of profound significance for both domestic and foreign policies in Russia.

We hope that the succeeding collections of papers on topics of equal importance will similarly contribute to improved mutual understanding and ongoing dialogue regarding the great questions of world affairs.

DOUGLAS C. LOVELACE, JR.
Director
Strategic Studies Institute

ABOUT THE CONTRIBUTORS

STEPHEN J. BLANK has served as the Strategic Studies Institute's expert on the Soviet bloc and the post-Soviet world since 1989. Prior to that he was Associate Professor of Soviet Studies at the Center for Aerospace Doctrine, Research, and Education, Maxwell Air Force Base, AL; and taught at the University of Texas, San Antonio; and at the University of California, Riverside. Dr. Blank is the editor of *Imperial Decline: Russia's Changing Position in Asia*, coeditor of *Soviet Military and the Future*, and author of *The Sorcerer as Apprentice: Stalin's Commissariat of Nationalities, 1917-1924*. He has also written many articles and conference papers on Russia, the Commonwealth of Independent States, and Eastern European security issues. Dr. Blank's current research deals with proliferation and the revolution in military affairs, and energy and security in Eurasia. His two most recent books are *Russo-Chinese Energy Relations: Politics in Command*, London, UK: Global Markets Briefing, 2006; and *Natural Allies? Regional Security in Asia and Prospects for Indo-American Strategic Cooperation*, Carlisle, PA: Strategic Studies Institute, U.S. Army War College, 2005. Dr. Blank holds a B.A. in history from the University of Pennsylvania, and an M.A. and Ph.D. in history from the University of Chicago.

THOMAS GOMART is currently the director of the Russia/NIS Centre at the French Institute of International Relations (IFRI) based in Paris and Brussels. He is the editor of the trilingual electronic collection *Russie. Nei.Visions*. Dr. Gomart's academic and professional background has been closely related to post-Soviet space. As Lavoisier Fellow at the State Institute for International Relations (University-MGIMO-Moscow); Visiting Fellow at the Institute for Security Studies (European Union-Paris); and Marie Curie Fellow at the Department of War Studies, King's College-London, Dr. Gomart has acquired a diversified international experience. He lectured on international affairs at the Special Military School of Saint-Cyr Coëtquidan (2002-2010). In 2008, he co-directed the IFRI/CSIS (Center for Strategic and International Studies) project *Europe, Russia, and the United States: Finding a New Balance.* Dr. Gomart's publications include *Russian Civil-Military Relations: Putin's Legacy* (Washington, DC, Carnegie Endowment for International Peace, 2008); *EU-Russia Relations: Toward a Way Out of Depression* (Washington, DC: IFRI/CSIS, 2008); and as editor, *Russie.Nei.Visions* (Paris, France: IFRI, 2009). He has also published various articles, including "L'Europe marginalisée," *Politique internationale*, n°118, 2008; "Russia Alone Forever? The Kremlin's Strategic Solitude," *Politique étrangère*, special issue WPC, 2008; "Washington-Moscou: la nouvelle donne" ("Washington-Moscow: The New Deal"), *Politique internationale*, n°123, 2009; "Obama and Russia : Facing the Heritage of the Bush Years," *Russie.Nei.Visions*, n°39, April 2009; "NATO-Russia: Is the 'Russian Question' European?" *Politique étrangère*, special issue, 4/2009; and "Europe in Russian Foreign Policy: Important but no longer Pivotal," *Russie.Nei.Visions*, n° 50, May 2010. Dr. Gomart holds an EMBA from HEC and a Ph.D. in history from Paris I Panthéon-Sorbonne.

INTRODUCTION

On January 25-26, 2010, the Strategic Studies Institute (SSI) organized a conference entitled, "Contemporary issues in International Security," at the Finnish embassy in Washington, DC. This was the second in what we hope will be annual conferences bringing together U.S., European, and Russian scholars and experts to discuss such issues in an open forum. The importance of such regular dialogues among experts is well known, and the benefits of these discussions are considerable. Just as we published the papers of the 2008 conference in 2009, (Stephen J. Blank, ed., *Prospects for U.S.-Russian Security Cooperation*, Carlisle, PA: Strategic Studies Institute, U.S. Army War College, 2009), we are doing so now. However, in this case, we are publishing the papers on a panel-by-panel basis.

The panel presented here was devoted to civil-military relations in Russia. This is, as the papers included here show, a critical topic in understanding the domestic and foreign policy trajectories of the Russian state. The papers provided here do not deny that civilian control exists. But they both show how highly undemocratic, and even dangerous, is the absence of those democratic controls over the military and the police forces in Russia which, taken together, comprise multiple militaries. These papers present differing U.S. and European assessments of the problems connected with civilian and democratic controls over the possessors of force in the Russian state and should stimulate further reflection upon these issues and those related to them.

Stephen J. Blank
Editor

CHAPTER 1

CIVIL-MILITARY RELATIONS AND RUSSIAN SECURITY

Stephen J. Blank

INTRODUCTION

The best recent scholarship on Russian civil-military relations explicitly addresses this issue's importance for both domestic and external security. Thomas Gomart has written that,

> Through the civil-military relationship the nature of a state's politico-strategic project can be assessed, that is, what is its understanding of the world; what resources does it have available, what is its willingness to modify its international environment. Studying the civil-military relationship also makes clear current modes of power, the sharing of responsibility in security matters, and in certain cases the will to act.[1]

Similarly, Zoltan Barany writes that,

> The reform of the armed forces is closely connected, through the broader issues of civil-military relations, to the general state of Russia's democratization. The politics of defense reform is at the core of Russia's democratization given the crucial role the military establishment has played throughout Russian history, including the more than seven decades of Communist rule during which the Soviet Union had built a great military empire.[2]

Thus an inquiry into the present state of those relations under conditions of defense reform and the current international situation is of immense analytical and policy relevance for both domestic and external security in Russia. Recent papers by this author and Dale Herspring have shown that while the Russian regime is serious about military reform, it is encountering severe objections from the uniformed military; and that second, the military has successfully persuaded the government to accept its expansive concept of the threats to Russia, i.e., its threat assessment.[3]

That threat assessment is one that postulates growing military threats from without, mainly from the United States and the North Atlantic Treaty Organization (NATO), an increased likelihood of the incidence of war, and, in general, a presupposition of political, if not military, conflict with the West that preserves the state of siege in world politics inaugurated by Vladimir Lenin. Moreover, this threat assessment also postulates increasing domestic threats to the security of the present political order and links those threats, as would a Leninist approach, to the same external adversaries, if not enemies, postulated in the external threat assessment. Yet despite this structural militarization of Russia's cognitive and policy approach to its security dilemmas, the military has only partly succeeded in convincing the government to accept its answers to these dilemmas. Those answers essentially entail returning to a form of mobilization even though defense spending, in a bow to the military, will reach unprecedented levels in 2010 despite the current economic crisis.[4]

This situation of inflated threat assessments leading to pro-military policy outcomes, even if they are only partially what the armed forces want, is a direct result of the enduring failure to establish democratic controls over the armed forces and the 18-year hiatus in defense reform since Mikhail Gorbachev's presidency in 1991. The implications for both domestic and external security policies are quite obvious. The constancy of such threat inflation and accusations of the West is another example of the consistent and clearly deliberate disinformation of the Russian government by its military and intelligence agencies, which is a fundamental outgrowth of the failure to control these agencies after 1991 by civilian and democratic means. As Pavel Felgenhauer, a leading defense correspondent, reports,

> Russia has a Prussian-style all-powerful General Staff that controls all the different armed services and is more or less independent of outside political constraints. Russian military intelligence – GRU, as big in size as the former KGB and spread over all continents – is an integral part of the General Staff. Through GRU, the General Staff controls the supply of vital information to all other decision-makers in all matters concerning defense procurement, threat assessment, and so on. High-ranking former GRU officers have told me that in Soviet times the General Staff used the GRU to grossly, deliberately, and constantly mislead the Kremlin about the magnitude and gravity of the military threat posed by the West in order to help inflate military expenditure. There are serious indications that at present the same foul practice is continuing.[5]

Similarly, in 2007 President Vladimir Putin told a press conference of Group of Eight (G-8) reporters that Russia and the West were returning to the Cold War, and added that,

> Of course we will return to those times. And it is clear that if part of the United States' nuclear capability is

situated in Europe and that our military experts consider that they represent a potential threat then we
will have to take appropriate retaliatory steps. What
steps? Of course we must have new targets in Europe.
And determining precisely which means will be used
to destroy the installations that our experts believe
represent a potential threat for the Russian Federation
is a matter of technology. Ballistic or cruise missiles or
a completely new system. I repeat that it is a matter of
technology.[6]

In other words, if the armed forces say something is
a threat, it is, regardless of an objective determination
of the merits of the case. Obviously under conditions of
autocracy, this is an invitation to the aforementioned
militarization of security policy and a posture based
on the presupposition of conflict. Consequently, it is
not surprising that analysts of the regime have noted
its propensity for conflict. As Andrei Illarionov writes,

Since its outset, the *Siloviki* regime has been aggressive. At first, it focused on actively destroying centers
of independent political, civil, and economic life within Russia. Upon achieving those goals, the regime's
aggressive behavior turned outward beyond Russia's
borders. At least since the assassination of the former
Chechen President Zelimkhan Yandarbiyev in Doha,
Qatar, on February 14, 2004, aggressive behavior by
SI [Siloviki] in the international arena has become the
rule rather than the exception. Over the last 5 years, the
regime has waged 10 different "wars" (most of them
involving propaganda, intelligence operations, and
economic coercion rather than open military force)
against neighbors and other foreign nations. The most
recent targets have included Ukraine [subjected to a
"second gas war" in early 2009], The United States
[subjected to a years-long campaign to rouse anti-
American sentiment], and, most notoriously, Georgia

[actually bombed and invaded in 2008]. In addition to their internal psychological need to wage aggressive wars, a rational motive is also driving the *Siloviki* to resort to conflict. War furnishes the best opportunities to distract domestic public opinion and destroy the remnants of the political and intellectual opposition within Russia itself. An undemocratic regime worried about the prospect of domestic economic social and political crises—such as those that now haunt Russia amid recession and falling oil prices—is likely to be pondering further acts of aggression. The note I end on, therefore, is a gloomy one: To me the probability that *Siloviki* Incorporated will be launching new wars seems alarmingly high.[7] (italics in original)

Illarionov's so-called wars also include "non-violent" conflicts and the possibility of heightened domestic repression using the instruments of force. Therefore, this chapter represents an inquiry into some of the consequences of this tense relationship for Russia's current domestic and external security. In this context, we must bear in mind that despite genuine reform, and even possibly because of it, the pathologies of Russia's civil-military relations have not yet been addressed, let alone overcome.

The Russo-Georgian war of 2008 reminded us that we neglect developments in Russian defense policy and overall military organization, to include the forces of the Ministry of Interior (VVMVD) and the intelligence services, at our peril. Two points stand out here. First, based on what we have already stated above, as a result of this war we should understand that we and Eurasia now live in a condition of permanent threat because Russian leaders are disposed towards the use of force under deliberately manufactured threat scenarios of constant ideological, information, and political, if not military threats of ideological and political war emanating from the West.[8]

Second, we cannot and are not arguing that Putin caused this war merely to retain his power and that of the structures of power (*Silovye Struktury*). The well-known geopolitical considerations that emerged before, during, and after combat operations cannot simply be called an appendage to the war. However, this crisis and war were clearly planned well in advance, and the provocation of Georgia was probably staged in such a way as to compel President Dmitri Medvedev, the sole person capable of legally authorizing force, to go beyond his initial support for a peace enforcement cooperation confined to South Ossetia to invade Georgia and detach its rebellious provinces from it.[9] Once the war began, it was clear that Putin took the leadership position from the first, not relinquishing the leadership until it became too obvious that he was usurping power. But few believe he has relinquished or lost it since the outbreak of hostilities. In other words, domestic considerations of primacy and place were probably not far from the calculations of Putin and his entourage.

Therefore we must closely follow those developments to understand more clearly current tendencies in Russian politics and policy as a whole. Specifically, this chapter examines issues pertaining to civil-military relations in several areas of Russian national security policies that suggest some disturbing trends for the future. These areas are the growing sense of the possible use of force against domestic potential opposition exacerbated by the current economic crisis; the pervasive corruption of the government and armed forces, which manifests itself not only in an outbreak of criminality within the government and military, but also in key areas of defense and foreign policy like arms sales; the potential for rivalry over defense and foreign policy in the so-called tandemocracy of President Dmitry Medvedev and Prime Minister Vladimir Putin; and the recent amendments to the Law on Defense concerning the use of Russia's armed forces abroad. All these phenomena have in common the fact that they not only demonstrate the dangers of what Medvedev has called "legal nihilism" to Russia's own security (and that of its partners and neighbors), but also that they are grounded in the very marrow of the Russian political system, namely this legal nihilism and increasing authoritarianism.

In other words, it is the lack of democratic controls on the use of force at home and abroad and the sheer unaccountability of Russia's government when it comes to use of those armed forces that are critical determining factors of Russia's political system. In no small measure, these factors are responsible for the fact that Russia continues to be a risk factor in international security, as Russian analysts themselves have long known.[10] Ultimately, it is Russia's system as much as, if not more than, any other government's policies towards Russia that is the fundamental problem for any analysis of Russian security. Bearing this context in mind, close examination of certain recent tendencies in defense and security policy reveals some ongoing trends that should either disturb us or at least compel close analysis of what they might portend for the future of Russian domestic and foreign policy. This is particularly true when we consider that Russia is currently undergoing a major military reform, the first real reform in years. That reform was announced immediately after the war with Georgia and was intended to remedy many of the shortcomings revealed by that war.

THE DOMESTIC SECURITY ISSUES OF
RUSSIAN DEFENSE

Not surprisingly, reform, despite its real progress, is encountering substantial opposition from the
military as well as the obstacles raised by the current
economic crisis that makes paying for it a much more
difficult proposition. There have been public demonstrations by uniformed military personnel who face
disbandment of their units, demands that Minister of
Defense Anatoly Serdyukov be fired, and visible public signs of military opposition in the media, hitherto
a rarity in Russia. This opposition itself testifies to one
dimension of the problem, the government's record
since 1991 of encouraging of open political activity or
politicization of the armed forces.[11] This opposition,
like the unrest generated by the current economic crisis, raises the possibility of large-scale manifestations
of unrest in Russia and of commensurate repression.

Indeed, some foreign analysts have opined that if
an order came to repress domestic opposition by force,
it might not be followed. Specifically, British analyst
Martin McAuley testified to Parliament that,

> In order to stay in power government needs the sup-
> port of security services. It is debatable if the military
> would now fully support the Putin Team given the
> disquiet over military reform. It might not be willing
> to shoot at Russian demonstrators. There are hints that
> middle FSB [Federal Security Service] officers are un-
> happy with the present state of affairs. In other words,
> the Putin Team cannot rely on the security services
> carrying out orders to use force against demonstra-
> tors.[12]

Similarly Vladimir Shlapentokh has written that,

If the Communists or any other political force in Russia brought to the streets of Moscow 10,000 to 20,000 people demanding the resignation of Russian leaders, the regime would be doomed. The notorious OMON [Special Purpose Police Unit], a special police unit which can easily deal with the gathering of a few hundred protesters in Moscow, would be helpless against mass demonstrations of this size. The Kremlin is unlikely to dispatch the order to spill blood dissimilar to the Iranian regime which did [so] recently. It is also very likely that the police or the army would be too afraid to obey such commands if they were issued. Therefore the Kremlin needs to prevent any mass protests by the opposition from happening in the first place.[13]

Alternatively, if the regime lurches towards greater authoritarianism it will depend even more on the armed forces and security services, and this, too, is a possibility that we cannot rule out.[14] That policy could lead not only to more repression and authoritarianism at home but also to a more aggressive foreign policy abroad, particularly in the Commonwealth of Independent States (CIS). Given the abundant signs of regime apprehension about domestic unrest in the current economic crisis and the elaborate efforts it makes to prevent a truly democratic election or open expression of public opinion, we can see that opportunities for the use of force against domestic opposition of any kind is a real prospect. Indeed, Felgengauer wrote that the military actively sought the right to use its forces, not the VVMVD, to quell domestic unrest should it break out.[15] Furthermore, as Barany observed, by virtue of the failure to democratize this issue Yeltsin, Putin, and now Medvedev have created a situation whereby they now stand face-to-face with the military, with only the instruments of personal control rather than a transparent, strong, legitimate government institution that can prevent even the danger of a coup or of internal violence.[16] Indeed, arguably one reason reform is so difficult is precisely the absence of such institutions in Russian politics, and that until the civil-military relationship is transformed, genuine reform will not occur.[17] There is ample evidence that both these dangers of unrest or of heightened forcible repression are growing, along with the authorities' perception of the manifestation of popular unrest due to the current economic crisis. Already in 2005-06 the Ministry of Defense (MoD) formed Special Designation Forces from Spetsnaz brigades under the Minister's direct control. They have air, marine, and ground components and conduct peace-support and counter-terrorist operations.[18] Since the minister answers only to the president, essentially this also means putting all Russia under threat of counterterrorist or other so-called operations without any Parliamentary accountability or scrutiny.

Since then matters have, if anything, grown worse. An April 2009 report outlined quite clearly the threat perceived by the authorities. Specifically it stated that,

> The Russian intelligence community is seriously worried about latent social processes capable of leading to the beginning of civil wars and conflicts on RF [Russian Federation] territory that can end up in a disruption of territorial integrity and the appearance of a large number of new sovereign powers. Data of an information "leak," the statistics and massive number of antigovernment actions, and official statements and appeals of the opposition attest to this.[19]

This report proceeded to say that these agencies expected massive protests in the Moscow area, industrial areas of the South Urals and Western Siberia, and in the Far East, while ethnic tension among the Muslims of the North Caucasus and Volga-Ural areas is also not excluded. The author also invoked the specter of enraged former Army officers and soldiers, who are now being demobilized because of the reforms, taking to the streets with their weapons. But despite the threat of this unrest, the government is characteristically resorting to strong-arm methods to meet this threat. In other words, it is repeating past regimes (not the least Yeltsin's) in strengthening the VVMVD and now other paramilitary forces as well.[20]

More soberly, this report, along with other articles, outlines the ways in which the internal armed forces are being strengthened. Special intelligence and commando subunits to conduct preventive elimination of opposition leaders are being established in the VVMVD. These forces are also receiving new models of weapons and equipment, as well as armored, artillery, naval, and air defense systems. In 2008, 5.5 billion rubles were allocated for these forces' modernization. Apart from the already permitted "corporate forces" of Gazprom and Transneft that monitor pipeline safety, the Ministry of Interior (MVD) is also now discussing an *Olimpstroi* (Olympics Construction) Army, and even the Fisheries inspectorate is going to create a special armed subunit called Piranha.[21]

Since then even more information about the extent of the domestic reconstruction of the MVD into a force intended to suppress any manifestation of dissent have emerged. As of 2003, there were 98 special-purpose police detachments (OMONs) in Russia. By comparison in 1988 during the crisis of the regime and its elites under Gorbachev, 19 OMONs were created in 14 Russian regions and three union republics. By 2007, there were already 121 OMON units comprising 20,000 men operating in Russia. Moreover, by

2007 there were another 87 police special designation detachments (OMSNs), with permanent staffing of over 5,200 people operating with the internal affairs organs, making a grand total of 208 special purpose or designated units with 25,000 well-trained and drilled soldiers. The OMSVs have grown from an anti-crime and anti-terrorist force to a force charged with stopping "extremist" criminal activity. All these units train together and have been centralized within the MVD to fight "organized crime, terrorism, and extremism." From 2005 to 2006, the financing of these units was almost doubled. By 2009, they were also working with aircraft assets, specifically the MVD's own Aviation Center with nine special purpose air detachments throughout Russia. Seven more such units are to be created. Furthermore, the MVD has developed a concept for rapidly airlifting these forces to troubled areas from other regions when necessary. These forces are also receiving large-scale deliveries of new armored vehicles with computers in some cases and command, control, and communications (C3) capabilities. Since these are forces apart from the regular VVMVD, "On a parallel basis with the OMON empire, a multi-level internal security troop machine is being developed-with its own special forces, aircraft, armored equipment, situational crisis centers, and so forth."[22] When one considers this huge expansion of the domestic *Silovye Struktury* (power organs), it becomes clear why already in 2008 Russia announced that it would increase funding for the Ministry of Interior by 50 percent in 2010 and where the government's estimation of the true threat to Russian security lies.[23]

Equally, if not more importantly, the quality, reliability, and extent of professionalism of the armed forces, as well as their responsiveness to civilian authority are crucial issues in Russia's defense and foreign policy. Since the Russian government is a highly autocratic one with little or no accountability of the Executive to anyone at home and is conducting an aggressive global foreign policy, these facts make the nature of the defense forces and defense policy a matter of urgent international and national interest. As McAuley concludes,

> The war in the Caucasus proves that Russian international behavior for the most part is decided by circles, which wittingly provokes Russia's defiant and aggressive international behavior with a view to restore a mobilized economy and its privileged status in the political system.[24]

However, even though the current military reform is both timely and essential if Russia is to have a modern army capable of defending against contemporary threats, it will not be sufficient if there is no reform of the pathetic state of civil-military relations that could threaten the state's integrity and stability if left unchecked. Here we should be blunt. After the fall of Communism 19 years ago, Russia has yet to create a system of civil-military relationships that provides effective control of both the government and the multiple armed forces. One result of this failure, as I have previously argued elsewhere, is that there exists within Russian politics and not exclusively within the armed forces, a constant temptation to use military force for the solution of problems that require a political resolution.[25] The second result of this enduring failure is no less and perhaps even more serious, namely the permanent tension, if not crisis, in civil-military relations is part of a larger and enduring crisis of the state. This tension, if not crisis, colors many if not all of Russia's security policies.

CORRUPTION AND CRIMINALITY

This second result is particularly visible if we take a broader and deeper analytical account of the rampant corruption within the multiple militaries, not to mention the state. After all, President Medvedev has made numerous efforts to launch a campaign against official corruption and complained more than once about what he calls Russia's legal nihilism, a phenomenon that is as much present in the defense and security sector as it is elsewhere. And preliminary signs show that despite now publicized efforts to uproot corruption and crime in the armed forces as a whole, again to include the VVMVD, in fact, despite the reform, the incidence of such events is rising. If this means reporting has improved, that is a welcome sign. But the current anti-corruption campaign has yet to land any truly big fish and in many ways reflects more the settling of clan scores atop the government machine than a commitment to living within the law.[26]

Even though we have long known of the corruption, criminality, venality, and brutality towards soldiers that pervades the entire military and despite years of publicity and promised efforts to uproot these trends, they evidently are worsening even as serious attempts are made to reform the armed forces. Ultimately, the pervasive corruption and criminality that we see in those forces reflect larger trends in the society and state as a whole. These incidences of corruption, lawlessness, criminality, and aggressiveness are profoundly significant because they can have wide-ranging, unpredictable, and even dangerous consequences for Russia and its overall policy, both domestic and foreign, that can add considerably to the already considerable number of security challenges that Russia both presents to the United States and that it also perceives. For example, it should be noted that when the Spanish police broke open a Russian Mafia mob in Spain in 2008, it turned out that the "Capos" of the Russian Mafia there were closely and personally tied to some of the highest ranking officials in the Russian government, e.g., winning lucrative public works contracts. Yet they also clearly had contacts with terrorists in the North Caucasus.[27] This should not be surprising, as by 2005 former Minister of the Interior Anatoly Kulikov was already warning of the criminalization of the state and the fusion of criminal and state organizations.[28]

In the security sphere, this issue became prominent as a result of the audit conducted by Defense Minister Sergei Ivanov in 2006-07. During the audit, Serdyukov discovered that corruption was even worse than expected. For example, on April 3, 2008, the Audit Chamber announced that more than 164.1 million rubles had been stolen from the ministry through fraud and outright theft. Another report stated that the MoD "accounts for 70 percent of the budgetary resources used for purposes other than those officially designated."[29] But while President Putin recognized the need for a new broom to sweep clean the Ministry and appointed Anatoly Serdyukov to do so, it is clear that despite Serdyukov's best efforts, corruption continued and is still going on.

Similarly, a recent audit revealed significant violations of financial and economic activity in the Air Force, amounting to a loss of over 660 million rubles. These violations occurred in the use of Air Force resources and funds by officials in Air Force commands, military units, and organizations.[30] In other words, this corruption pervaded the Air Force. And this pervasiveness embraces the entire armed forces as well, not just the Air Force. Thus in 2008 Russia's leading defense correspondent, Alexander Golts, told a U.S. audience that 30-50 percent of the annual defense spending in Russia is simply stolen.[31] More recently, prosecutors uncovered mass fraud in *Rosoboronzakaz* (Russian State Defense Purchasing Agency) in the amount of 6.5 billion rubles, as well as the unlawful spending of 1.3 billion rubles and the inappropriate use of funds of 98 million rubles.[32] From January-August 2009 alone, an investigation uncovered 1,343 violations of the law on the placement of defense orders in *Rosoboronzakaz*.[33] Indeed, an earlier investigation in June by the Main Military Prosecutor's office revealed about 3000 violations, costing the state another 380 million rubles, leading a commentator to observe that some these criminal schemes were notable not just for their scope, but for their brazenness—"one gets the impression that these persons were not afraid of anything."[34]

Under the circumstances, we should not be surprised that the Russian armed forces are not receiving modern weapons (although corruption is not the only reason for this failure). Another recent audit revealed that, "At present the share of the modern types of weapons and hardware that are supplied to the Russian army and navy is not more than 6 percent." And the situation in the high-tech sectors of the military—ships, missiles, and space hardware—is especially difficult.[35] Insofar as the defense reform's ultimate success is predicated on the effective production and distribution through the armed forces of modern weapons, this failure jeopardizes the defense reform.

Likewise, in the Ministry of Interior Minister Rashid Nurgaliyev recently gave regional law enforcement chiefs a month to clear out the corruption in their midst or be sacked for failure to control their units or because they, too, are implicated in the corruption. Nurgaliyev revealed that in the first 6 months of 2009, 274 criminal proceedings have been launched against Ministry Chiefs at various levels, leading in some cases to outright dismissals. In addition, the investigation uncovered 44,000 violations by law enforcement officials, involving 2,500 crimes committed by law enforcement agency employees.[36]

That aforementioned attitude of not fearing anything exemplifies the scope of the problem, even though it is clear that there is now pressure to uncover such cases. And the corruption of the government as a whole in Russia needs no explication here in view of the widely decried fact of this corruption by President Medvedev and numerous commentators. Indeed, these cases show that some sense of the scope of this criminality is now becoming public as part of Medvedev's campaign, which has been reinvigorated insofar as the military is concerned. Arguably, Medvedev's failure to date to uproot this pervasive criminality is what has led to the recent disclosures of corruption in numerous sectors of state and military activity. For example, in the military recent figures show that the number of crimes committed by the military during 2008 rose by 9 percent, and the crime rate in the military was the highest among the security related agencies in Russia (this is what is in the report, and given the notorious corruption of the police, this is a frightening claim). Military prosecutors completed investigations of 12,000 crimes and brought 80 percent of cases to court, including 12 cases against high-ranking military officers.[37] And in the first half of 2009, military investigators completed proceedings of 6,296 crimes, almost 10 percent more than in 2008, while there are also reports of falling crime rates in the Ministry of Emergency Situations and the Ministry of Interior.[38] Nevertheless, the number of cases in this sector involving the abuse of authority for "mercenary" reasons is increasing, as is the overall military crime rate.[39]

Subsequently, in July 2009, the Chief Military Prosecutor announced that crimes committed by officers had reached "unprecedented levels." During 2008, officers had committed 4,159 crimes, including 1,754 corruption-related offenses, a 38 percent increase over 2007. Meanwhile, already by June 2009 they had committed over 2,000 crimes, or one in four of total crimes, an increase of 7 percent on a year-on-year basis. While many of these crimes involve physical assaults on service personnel (over 5,430 personnel reporting such assaults); one-third of the crimes involved corruption. Since 2004, the number of Russian generals and admirals prosecuted for corruption had increased by almost seven times.[40] Official figures calculate that these cases of corruption resulted in losses of at least 2.2 billion rubles ($78.6 million) to the state budget in 2008.[41] Finally the evidence of the military forces and its leadership's collusion with organized crime is also now coming to light. The U.S. Cyber Consequences Unit recently reported to the U.S. Government that,

> Denial of service and web defacement attacks launched last year against Georgian web sites were carried out by Russian civilians and sympathizers rather than the government but were coordinated with the invasion of the former Soviet state and had the cooperation of both the Russian Army and organized crime, according to a report being released today to U.S. government officials.[42]

This connection, unfortunately, is not so surprising, given the extensive reporting of the links between major energy firms like the notorious *Rosukrenergo*, a key middleman in Russo-Ukrainian gas deals, and leading figures of Russian organized crime, and similar such links throughout Eastern Europe.[43]

If we assume that cases that are uncovered are only a fraction of the sum total of criminal activity in any organized social environment, it becomes clear that we are witnessing the overall degradation of the Russian military and government. It is not too much to say, as do many European governmental analysts and officials, that we see a criminal, if not Mafia, state (their term).[44] Indeed, no military organization is so isolated from the state and society that its degradation does not both imply and rebound back upon the overall degeneration of that state and society. For example, recent investigations have uncovered figures that were shocking, even to the Russian government, concerning the brutality and venality of the police forces and the level of criminal violations among them.

> According to the available statistics, the law enforcement [agencies] are far ahead of the other corruption-prone bodies of power. In 2008, 3,329 police were punished for bribes, in contrast to 433 employees in the health service and 378 in education. According to police, 2,516 crimes committed by police and federal migration service personnel have been identified in January-July, including 1,600 cases of abuse of office.[45]

This last charge that amounts to the criminalization of the state is not as surprising as it may seem, for Russian and foreign observers have long pointed to the integration of criminal elements with both the energy, intelligence, and defense industrial sectors of the economy and as an instrument of Russian foreign policy in Eastern Europe.[46] Accordingly, summarizing a great deal of evidence, Janusz Bugajski observes that such criminal penetration of Central and Eastern Europe, including the members of the CIS is a major security concern to those governments because these criminal networks both destabilize their host countries and render services to political interests in Moscow.

> The Russian *Mafiya* greatly expanded its activities throughout the region during the 1990s and established regional networks in such illicit endeavors as drug smuggling, money laundering, international prostitution, and migrant trafficking. In some countries, Russian syndicates have been in competition with local gangs, while in others they have collaborated and complemented each other. Analysts in the region contended that Russian intelligence services coordinated several criminal groups abroad and directed a proportion of their resources to exert economic and political influence in parts of Eastern Europe.[47]

Bugajski's observations correspond to the findings of many other researchers and East European officials concerning the linkages among business, state, intelligence, and organized crime. Thus it has long been known that throughout Eastern Europe and the CIS that the Russian state, intelligence services, energy firms, and organized crime, all collaborate together on behalf of Russian interests. As the record shows, they seek to gain access to legitimate business firms, control key sectors of the economy and newsmedia, subvert political parties, and buy political influence and politicians throughout the region.[48]

Because of the fact that, as Dmitry Trenin has remarked, "Russia is governed by the people who own it," office and property, as in medieval times and in the Soviet *Nomenklatura*, are one and the same. Power leads to wealth and property, and vice versa. Indeed, it cannot be otherwise in such a system. And since this is a system that has systematically freed the executive from any accountability to the news media, Parliament or anyone else and therefore lacks a concept of the rule of law or of the sanctity of contracts and private property, this outcome is hardly surprising. Recent reports in the Russian press give some indication of the scope of the problem. Medvedev himself has announced what everyone knew, namely that official positions are bought and sold.[49]

Thus this criminality is not confined to the armed forces or security sector, but rather it epitomizes the way in which governing occurs throughout the state. Indeed, Dmitri Simes and Paul Saunders recently called it the glue that holds together the disparate groups that constitute Russia's governing elite.[50] But beyond that Simes, Saunders, and Russian analysts alike point out that this pervasive corruption not only impedes foreign and domestic investment, it solidifies a dysfunctional political system where the elite has little genuine concern for the national interest or capability to formulate it and is instead busy feathering its own nest.[51] As Vyacheslav Glazychev writes,

> The way Russia is now run clearly reflects Putin's personality and management style. First, there is a linear scheme of administration, based on the idea of the "vertical," rather than a rule-applying bureaucracy. Second, mutual loyalty forms the basis for selecting one's "team" and is combined with open contempt for the government structure itself. Third, the principle of unilateral command from above combines eclectically with some elements of economic liberalism.[52]

The behavior described here perfectly conforms to this depiction of the current governing reality in both the defense sector and throughout the state as a whole. To overcome this sign of pervasive anomic behavior among the security services and sector, we must also overcome it in the state, a tall and dubious order. But it is obvious that the continuation of such trends can only further enfeeble the central government's ability to modernize Russia, let alone reform or democratize it. Moreover, it is fraught with dangerous implications for Russia; Russia's internal, if not external, security; and its armed forces.

First, this widespread criminality provides powerful disincentives to reforming the conditions that make soldiers the easy prey of veterans and officers. And the uprooting of such phenomena as *Dedovshchina* (hazing), enserfment of soldiers, theft, and violence against them by superior officers and veterans is essential to any successful defense reform, which, after all, aims at creating a so-called professional army. Despite the reforms to date, it is still clear that these phenomena remain and pose a serious problem within the armed forces. Indeed, the reforms during the first 6 months of 2009 did not lead to a reduction in the incidence of crime or corruption within the armed forces. If anything, these manifestations increased.[53] This is not only a question of crime and corruption but of hazing and violence, including torture against soldiers by officers, suicides, and other noncombat deaths.[54] Military spokesmen suggest that this problem may continue because even as the officer corps is downgraded, those remaining are not trained or equipped to deal with a new army, and others may resist losing their perquisites. Worse yet, in 2009 figures suggest that not only is the Russian army drafting people with a criminal record for the first time in this decade, but that their number amounts to more than half of those drafted since autumn 2008.[55] While the government is now introducing chaplains for the armed forces to introduce some form of moral counseling and attempting other procedural reforms to stop this trend, if the new army remains a home for criminals and brutes, that will defeat the entire purpose of the reform.

More grandly, this widespread brutality and corruption lead the military leadership, much of which directly benefits from this state of affairs, to resist reforms and create powerful obstacles to reforms that would lead to a genuinely modern, and truly professional army where soldiers have enforceable legal rights and recourse against accountable colleagues and officers rather than perpetuate the continuing treatment of enlisted men as serfs and "baptized property" (the term coined by 19th century dissident Alexander Herzen to describe serfs). Moscow's earlier inability and refusal to reform its military, end conscription, and institute a genuinely professional military leads to an armed force composed of the uneducated; physically, morally, and mentally unfit; and widespread brutality and corruption, which militates against an army that can, except for certain specialized forces, effectively use high-tech weaponry. Under the circumstances, it is not surprising that Chief of Staff General Nikolai Makarov openly admitted in 2008 that the army was not ready for 21st century warfare.[56] And this was hardly the only set of reasons why the army was so backward compared to contemporary requirements.

Certainly the pervasiveness of these pathologies precludes creation of a truly professional army in any sense of the word. This is not merely a question of men and women being paid well for their services to the state, nation, and military. It also is a question of inculcating in the armed forces the sense of professionalism, of belonging to a profession with a genuine ethic of patriotic service. This ethic, arguably is that of a profession not that of a bureaucracy, although in Russia's case, while we have the pathologies of bureaucratic procedure and an immense state, we certainly do not even have a bureaucracy in the sense of a disinterested and nonpartisan corps of public servants. As a result, the whole notion that commanding officers can lead the armed forces in such a way as to inculcate this professionalism and an ethic of it among the men under their command flies out the window. Instead, we have an army like the one seen in Georgia and described above by Makarov. [57]

Yet at the same time, the reform has paradoxically given a new impetus to corruption and criminality within the armed forces that may help explain the rise of such incidents, even as the reform is occurring. Marc Galeotti offers the following reasons for the new impetus towards corruption. The reform takes place in a context of constantly rising defense appropriations, including for 2010. Much of this will go to the reform, specifically raising salaries and professionalization, i.e., the "recruitment" of "professional" soldiers at higher rates of pay and improved conditions and housing. Already some officers receive bonuses that triple or quadruple their basic pay. Consequently, officers are scrambling for bonuses and to avoid dismissal as the armed forces downsize.[58]

> This has created massive opportunities for corruption. Senior officers and those within the personnel directorates can demand and expect substantial bribes for their recommendations. According to some Defense Ministry sources, the going rate can be the equivalent

of a full year's salary in return for guaranteeing continued employment on the higher pay scale. Furthermore, the Defense Ministry is gearing up for a massive campaign of refurbishing and replacing rundown barracks and other facilities. This opens up opportunities for a wide range of money-making ventures from selling off second-hand furniture and equipment (which is then logged as having been destroyed) to manipulating bidding by contractors to secure government contracts.[59]

And the continuing insurgencies in the North Caucasus contribute greatly to this state of affairs.

If crimes by officers throughout the country in general hold to their normal level, meaning that every fourth criminal is an officer, then, in the 42nd Motorized Rifle Division, which deployed to Chechnya, the situation is much worse, with more than half the crimes in the unit committed by the officer corps. The situation is also bad in the Airborne Troops, the Space Troops, the Air Force, the Volga-Urals Military District, North Caucasus Military District, and the Moscow garrison. There almost a third of all crimes reported last year was committed by officers.[60]

Crime is not limited to lower and mid-level officers. The same source noted that "In 2004, only three generals were tried, but in 2008, 20 were." The bottom line is that officer crimes are out of control. "The crime rates are the highest over the past 10 years. Officers are responsible for more than 2,000 crimes with one-third of these linked to corruption."[61]

Thus pervasive corruption, criminality, and brutality have become major causes of Russia's inability to deal effectively with the mounting threats in the North Caucasus, as they are helping to turn the local population away from Moscow and to the Islamic fundamentalists who are leading the revolts against Russian rule. Any objective account of this insurgency cannot overlook the seriousness of the Islamic threat and its equal levels of violence and terror against the population.[62] Nevertheless, the fact remains that every fifth incident in the Army involves servicemen from the North Caucasus, where indeed there is no problem recruiting soldiers. Obviously, the potential material rewards of service plus the martial traditions of the region are attractive to local men, especially as this remains the poorest region of Russia. Indeed, men are now bribing recruiters to get into the service in an ironic reversal of past practice that involved bribes to be exempted.[63] These soldiers bring their own culture and a propensity for ethnic organization of parallel discipline structures into the army, leading to violence, discipline problems, interethnic conflicts within units, and, of course, criminality. But if the Russian army continues to experiment with ethnic-based units, it runs the risk of intensifying the problems already discerned here.[64]

In the case of the Caucasus, there are already abundant reports that Russian armed forces, (it is unclear if this is the regular army or the VVMVD) operate as death squads. This phenomenon is of long-standing and grows out of the long war in Chechnya. It also appears to be a pervasive phenomenon throughout the North Caucasus. Such operations are particularly centered in the units of the various Special Forces operating there and are looked on with a blind eye by higher authorities.[65] They kidnap and kill people with seeming impunity, and Russian human rights organizations suggest that there exists a correlation between this violence and the rising tide of insurgency in both Chechnya in particular, and the North Caucasus as a whole.[66] Aleksandr' Cheraskov of Memorial (the organization established to preserve a living memory of Stalin's crimes) observed that these death squads target young men of military age, which only makes them more susceptible to recruitment by rebel groups.[67] And Ludmilla Alexeyeva, the head of the Moscow Helsinki Group said,

> What we see now in all these (Caucasus) republics is a civil war between the security forces and the clandestine fighters, and between the security forces and the local population. . . . In the end we will lose the North Caucasus. The Russian president doesn't wish this, of course, but he has no control over his own security forces.[68]

And that is precisely the point. After 10 years of unsparing brutality on all sides in Chechnya, that province, as well as its neighbors, is aflame, with no end to these conflicts in sight. Much of this is directly traceable to the violence and corruption of the Russian armed forces that continually undermines the real security of the Russian Federation and which itself is only a partial manifestation of the larger and even more endemic corruption and brutality of the government.

The Shamanov Affair.

The threats to the state from this degeneration of the Russian military became painfully clear in September 2009 in what might be called the Shamanov affair. General Vladimir Shamanov is a two-star general and commander in chief of the Russian airborne forces (VDV). His daughter and son-in-law, Alexei

Khramyshin, are the owners of the Sporttek business that leases commercial space out to other businesses in Moscow, and his son, Yuri, is a member of its board. This business has clear connections to organized crime.[69] Shamanov's daughter and, especially his son-in-law, are under investigation for organizing an attempted murder of a businessman in 2006, and Khramyshin is the object of an international arrest warrant even though he remains at large. Khramyshin is also believed to be a high-ranking member in the Tatar crime gang.[70] On August 18, 2009, upon learning that the authorities were searching Sporttek's office, General Shamanov called up VDV Colonel Vadim Pankov and ordered him to send two detachments of VDV Special Forces to the office in Moscow and to detain and intern the special investigator and seal the building. Upon learning of this move, the investigator cut short his search and left, and the troops returned to their base. Since the call was taped as part of the larger investigation, the tapes were released a few weeks later, causing an uproar.[71]

Ironically, Shamanov has been a forceful exponent of the defense reform, making himself a prominent target for those who oppose it. But his misadventures reveal all the dangers of corruption we have outlined above. First, the investigation of Sporttek reveals the intimate links between members of organized crime syndicates and key military commanders. Second, it shows Shamanov used his authority to quash an investigation or part of one of this organized crime activity. But most dangerously, Shamanov's actions exposed the fiction of state control over the armed forces that Alexeyeva warned about. Russian political authorities have always possessed a heightened sensitivity to the specter of Bonapartism, a coup by a general, and Shamanov's ability to order troops on his own authority into Moscow for nonmilitary purposes without any accountability whatsoever, raised that specter in the most brazen and overt manner possible.[72] As Felgenhauer commented about this affair, it displayed the lack of control over the military.

> The fact that paratroopers were ordered into Moscow and actually moved in without the consent (or knowledge-author) of the Kremlin or government has revealed a serious lack of political control. Russia is an authoritarian state with no serious civil control over its military. If Putin and the Putin-appointed President Dmitry Medvedev also cannot control military movements even within Moscow, a coup in Russia is possible. Of course, Shamanov on August 18 was not contemplating launching a coup, but apparently using paratroopers to defend his business interests. However, if such things are allowed, Shamanov or another general (colonel) might in the future use Special Forces to arrest Putin, or Medvedev, or both. Within Moscow, a relatively small troop of determined, well trained, and armed soldiers could do it. The radical military reform in Russia is aimed at creating a more modern, mobile standing armed force, and its men are increasingly dependent on their commanders for their well being.[73]

Not only does this assessment reinforce Galeotti's insight into why reform should make corruption flourish, it also ties together the links between organized crime, the armed forces as a whole, their corruption, and the possibility of a military takeover. In view of the pervasive legal and moral nihilism of the system, including all the security services and the politicization of the Russian military that observers have already noted in earlier studies, this affair underscores many of the dangers confronting Russia from its own armed forces.[74]

Corruption in Arms Sales.

Any state's arms sales policy stands at the intersection of its foreign and domestic policies because it links the effective organization of its defense sector (a large and critical part of the overall economy) to the pursuit of defense and foreign policy goals. And this is certainly the case with Russia. In this context, one of the most dangerous aspects of the pervasive corruption discussed above is its equally pervasive presence in arms sales. This is not merely a discussion of the use of shadowy intermediaries and arms brokers like Viktor Bout, but rather the systematic corruption of the topmost leaders of the government. Again, we must reiterate that the point is not that Russia conducts so-called "black operations" abroad (many states do), but rather that its political and military leadership has a personal and pecuniary interest in arms sales, and that the defense sector has long been one penetrated by organized crime and corruption that links itself to the conduct of sensitive state policies with ensuing dangrous consequences.

The available evidence clearly suggests that these activities are widespread and that Bout and his analogues abroad have excellent contacts with high-ranking Russian officials with responsibility in the security sphere. Such activities are also of long-standing. In such a system, opacity, even if we were not in the naturally secretive defense sector, is the rule, not the exception. Accountability in this sector is limited at best, and corruption is ubiquitous. In fact, one might argue that corruption and criminality are rampant throughout the entire economy.[75] Similarly, another recent commentary observed, "In Russia corruption is the strongest vertical structure, on which the entire state arrangement is based."[76] Already in 2003, Federal Security Service (FSB) Director Nikolai Patrushev indicated his concern at the extent of criminal penetration of defense industry and hinted that his organization might have to intervene (no doubt to take the action away from the criminals to it and its friends).[77] Indeed, as the Russian press and Russian scholars and observers like Leonid Kosals and Vitaly Shlykov have often observed, Russia's defense industry is pervaded by corruption and even criminal violence, including forcible seizures of companies and even the murders of executives of defense firms in the competition for control over the rents accruing from arms sales either to the Russian army or abroad.[78]

For example, Russia's controls over the missiles that it has sold to Syria and Iran also proved to be remarkably porous, as many of them went to Hezbollah in 2000-06, and probably since then as well.[79] And there is good reason to believe that there is much hardware going to dangerous states from Russia through third parties or other unaccountable middlemen like Bout. Already in July, 2000 *Kommersant* reported that,

> The world community has long treated Belarus as a sickly child, of whom few demands are made, that had previously been exploited by Russia, which under U.S. pressure had to abandon direct cooperation in the military sphere with Iran. Russian military-industrial complex output started reaching the Iranians via our Belarusian brothers, who had few commitments to Washington [and this was during the Gore-Chernomyrdin agreement's operation-author] Cooperation between Minsk and Baghdad has been developing

rapidly of late. Official statistics confirm that Belarusian-Iraqi trade turnover in 1999 came to $6 million. According to Kommersant's information, that indicator was understated at least 10-fold.[80]

There is good reason to believe that similar machinations with regard to conventional missiles (*Iskander*) have continued. For example, in September 2009 Russian customs officers in *Krasnodar* prevented the smuggling of spares for the MiG-29 Fighter to Syria.[81] Scandals involving Ukraine's transfer of Russian missiles have occurred and, as shown below, there is good reason to believe that similar events are continuing insofar as Russian supplies to Syria are concerned. And the scale of gray or black market transfers to would-be proliferators cannot be known.

For example, the activities of international arms brokers like Bout expose loopholes in international agreements and conventions to which Russia and many other states are a party. These brokers have established networks of international arms sales that span continents and also apply to technologies usable for weapons of mass destruction (WMD).[82] Some of the examples of corruption may be gleaned from an anlysis of Russian arms sales to Venezuela. In 2008, Bout was arrested in Thailand as part of a sting organized by the U.S. Government. Interestingly enough, he was arrested for offering to deliver weapons to Colombia's rebel army, the Revolutionary Armed Forces of Colombia (FARC), who are also implicated in the drug trade. It may not be a coincidence, but Bout's offers coincide with what is clearly a Russian effort to inflame Latin America in a further internal and external conflict involving Venezuelan and Ecuadorian support for the FARC against the U.S. ally, Colombia.[83]

After Bout was arrested in Thailand, Moscow lobbied for his return to Russia, where he had lived freely in spite of an international warrant for his arrest. Western analysts suspect he has close ties to Russia's military and intelligence forces, as Bout had admitted carrying air shipments for the Russian state. Russian Foreign Minister Sergei Lavrov asked the authorities in Bangkok to make sure the hearing was held "impartially, without politicization." Moscow brought immense pressure to bear upon Bangkok so that he would not be extradited to the United States and forced to name names, dates, places, etc.[84] Moscow also increased incentives to Thailand not to extradite Bout. Russia sold cheap oil to Thailand last year and is in talks to sell fighter jets. Former Director of Operations for the Drug Enforcement Agency (DEA) Michael Braun, who oversaw the operation against Mr. Bout, told the *Financial Times* that he had received "a great deal of information over the past few months that attempts were under way by Russia to buy Bout's way out." Mr. Braun, now a security consultant, added, "The last thing they wanted was for him to be on U.S. soil where he could open up."[85] And we should note that Bout is hardly the only international arms broker involved in running weapons to the FARC or to other criminal, insurgent, and terrorist groups in Latin America.[86]

Undoubtedly Moscow also fully recognizes President Hugo Chavez's conversion of Venezuela into a critical transshipment center for narcotics from both Latin America and West Africa, along with his support for insurgencies and terrorists throughout Latin America. He has expansionist and revolutionary dreams about Colombia and seeks to exploit those factors for his own anti-American purposes.[87] Indeed, reports from 2003 point to Russian criminal penetration of Mexico's narcotics gangs.[88] More recently, in early 2009 a Russian and Cuban citizen were both arrested for drug smuggling in Yucatan.[89]

Apart from gaining cash for the defense sector, these purchases make no strategic sense for Russia. That is, unless they are intended for other purposes, e.g., helping the FARC and other similar groups fighting in Colombia, power projection throughout Latin America, drug running with submarines and protection of them against air attacks, or providing a temporary base for Russian naval and air forces where they can be sheltered from attacks but threaten North or South America.[90] Russia also supports the allegedly peaceful Venezuelan development of nuclear energy and the discovery of uranium and thorium there.[91] Iran is now actively helping Venezuela explore for uranium.[92] These developments suggest the possiblity of Venezuela functioning as a kind of swing man or pivot for a Russo-Venezuelan-Iranian alliance against the United States. Certainly elements in the Iranian press and government believe that Tehran should further intensify its already extensive efforts to create the possibility of a "second front" in political, or even in military, terms against the United States. Hezbollah already raises money and runs drugs in Latin America, and many have noted the growing network of ties between Iran and Latin American insurgents and terrorists facilitated by Chavez.[93] It is difficult to see how this benefits Russia in any serious way other than by simply making life difficult for Latin Americans and the United States. But as Lenin (who should have known this) remarked, "spite, in general, plays the very worst role in politics."

Iran offers an even more dangerous example of what happens when the arms sales business beomes enmeshed with high-level corruption leading the criminalization of state policy. The recent incident of the *Arctic Sea*, a ship that reportedly left Russia and was suposedly hijacked by pirates in the Baltic Sea and disappeared until the Russian Navy tracked it down in the Cape Verde Islands, illustrates that the cancer of corruption in the arms trade has apparently infected Russian arms sales to Iran. More and more, it looks like this ship was chartered to run Russian missile parts to Iran, indicating an extensive network of corruption throughout the arms sales and military industrial complex establishments. Allegedly, the Israeli Mossad discovered this sale and tipped off Russian intelligence, so as not to embarrass Russia.[94] But this situation embodies the dangerous link between the Russian arms mafia and the government, including corrupt officials and middlemen. As an Israeli columnist wrote recently,

> In modern-day Russia, there really does exist a symbiosis between the state and the weapons mafia. In this situation, the mafia does not always have to act in circumvention of the state machine to supply weapons to pariah states. The mafia—and this might be the most important conclusion to be drawn from the story of the disappearnce of the notorious freighter (*Arctic Sea*-author)—can be used as a weapon for state policy. Clearly, the Russian government will not dare use official channels today to supply missile systems to Iran. However, when it is the mafia at work, illegally selling these systems, well, what can the government do when it is certain that merely lumber is being exported from the country?[95]

Even more serious charges have surfaced since then in a report by the leftist *forum.msk.ru* newspaper. It alleges that the Russian government, operating through the GRU led by General Valentin Korabel'nikov, put together a decade-long program of clandestine weapons sales to Iran to keep Israel and Washington guessing as to Iran's true capabilities. This gray and black market program also enlisted the cooperation of the governments of Algeria and Syria, the arms brokers Viktor Bout and Munzer al-Kassar (who was arrested in Spain in 2007 and since extradited to the United States), and Russian organized crime figures in Spain, along with members of the Kurdistan Workers' Party (PKK) who have bases in Iran and engage regularly in arms trafficking. In other words, Moscow orchestrated a long-running program of illicit and clandestine arms sales to Iran, involving terrorists, criminals, and complicit governments until the network began to break down with the arrests of Kurdish contact Zakhar Kalashov, thanks to the efforts, among others, of Anatoly Litvinenko who was murdered in 2006, probably by Russian intelligence. That initial arrest led to other arrests, the breakup of the program, Algeria's return of Russian weapons, allegedly because they were defective, the sacking of General Korabel'nikov, the breakup of the network with the arrests of the two arms brokers, and an abortive last attempt, using the *Arctic Sea* to run weapons to Iran in 2009.[96] If these reports are true, they would represent the depths of corruption to which the arms trade has brought the government in its linkages with organized crime, also a fact of life in the government's energy business, and illustrate the dangers this trade poses to Moscow, and to international security more generally.

Since Iran then reexports these weapons, including possibly Shahab-3 missiles to other rogue states like Syria or terrorist groups, this amounts to playing with fire.[97] This urge to play with fire and also to be on both sides of the action in the Middle East is not new. We have seen it earlier in Iraq. Before the invasion of Iraq in 2003, Russia simultaneously sought partnership with Washington; a free hand at home, and in the CIS against terrorists; and friendship with Iraq. It was prepared to look the other way if Washington took account of Russian interests in Iraq, more broadly the Gulf, and the CIS because those interests were both economic and political and because they served to enrich key political elites in Moscow and validate Russia's stance as a legitimate actor regarding Iraq's destiny beyond Russia's membership in the United Nations (UN) Security Council. Those interests included large debts of $7-8 billion, large-scale energy contracts to develop Iraqi oil fields, large-scale trade in Russian goods under the notoriously corrupt oil for food program that, as we now know, enriched many members of Russia's top elite. Beyond that the Gulf states in general were and are regarded by two of Russia's most prominent lobbies after energy, defense industry, and the Ministry of Atomic Affairs (Minatom), as fertile hunting grounds for large profitable sales.[98] At the same time, Russian intelligence was furnishing Saddam with the results of Western conversations about Iraq and running weapons to Iraq, again indicating Moscow's desire to keep a foot in both camps.[99]

Meanwhile, for over a decade Moscow has been the main provider of external support for Iran's missile, air defense, space, and navy programs.[100] This cooperation goes back a long way. In 1998, Yevgenia Albats outlined Russo-Iranian collaboration in helping Iran build nuclear missiles for use as a future intermediate range ballistic missile (IRBM) to target Israel and Turkey. Iran also hopes to build an intercontinental ballistic missile (ICBM) to target the United States and Europe. Albats detailed the conscious participation and coordination of Russia's FSB, the State Commissions on Non-Proliferation, and on Science and Technology, Yevgeny Primakov's Ministry of Foreign Affairs, and probably the MoD in projects to send Russian scientists to Iran to transfer nuclear know-how as Iran seeks to develop IRBMs and then ICBMs.[101] The large number of Russian scientific-technological institutions helping Iran develop its programs strongly suggests governmental involvement in coordinating this interaction, especially as many of them either have close connections with the government, or are under its authority, or claim to have informed the government of what they were selling to Iran.[102]

The known technology transfers of WMD to Iran involve production technology and testing of the rocket engine for the SS-4 missile in violation of the missile technology control regime (MTCR), the reactor at Bushehr, as well as the continuing exchange of scientific know-how with Iranian scientists and/or training in Russia for them.[103] Because the SS-4 is ineffective and inaccurate with small payloads, it must have mass destruction payloads and capability to be effective.[104] The Bushehr reactor comprises four reactors plus turbines that Russia is now expected to provide along with more military technology and weapons since Ukraine dropped out under U.S. pressure. All this assistance occurs even though Russian officials know and publicly admit Iran is building nuclear weapons.[105] To be sure, Russia has clearly delayed indefinitely the completion of Bushehr, indicating its knowledge of Iranian policy, but the record of the past still stands. Indeed, the Russian press publicly acknowledged that the Shihab-3 is built with the latest Russian technology.[106]

Now the Russian government realizes it might have a problem. Certainly, its armed forces understand that there is a growing Iranian missile, satellite, and nuclear threat. Both Ivanov and former Chief of Staff General Yuri N. Baluyevsky have acknowledged Iran's threats.[107] Commenting on Iran's launch in early 2007 of a sub-orbital weather rocket, Lieutenant General Leonid Sazhin stated that,

> Iran's launch of a weather rocket shows that Tehran has not given up efforts to achieve two goals — create its own carrier rocket to take spacecraft to orbit and real medium-range combat missiles capable of hitting targets 3,000-5,000 miles away.[108]

Sazhin also warned that Iran was thereby developing capabilities that could strike Russia and Europe and trying to create its own missile carrier to orbit both satellites and medium range-missiles.[109] Although he argued that this capability would not fully materialize for 3-5 years, it would also take at least that long to test and deploy the American missile defenses that are at issue. Likewise, Major-General Vitaly Dubrovin, a Russian space defense expert, said flatly "now Tehran has a medium-range ballistic missile, capable of carrying a warhead" and admitted that this threatens everyone, including Russia.[110] Naturally both men lamented Iran's decision to validate U.S. threat assessments.[111] Mikhail Margelov, Chairman of the Federation Council's Foreign Affairs Committee, admitted that one could not rule out that Iran's nuclear program may have a future military nature.[112] Since February 2007, Iran has developed the Ashura IRMB, with a 2,000 kilometer (km) range, and the Sajil solid fuel missile with comparable range.[113]

By midsummer 2008, General Victor Yesin, First Vice-President of the Security, Defense, and Law and Order Academy, opined that by 2016-18 Iran might be able to create ICBMs.[114]

> Iran continues developing its program and, in the very near future, we should expect that missiles with a medium range of up to 4,000 kilometers will be created. The recently tested Shihab-3 missile is different from Korean counterparts. Its engine has been developed by Iranian specialists. As regards intercontinental missiles, they will appear in Iran no sooner than after eight-ten years.[115]

In August 2008, commenting on Iran's launch of the Safir missile, Moscow's Foreign Ministry spokesman Andrei Nesterenko decried "unwarranted" speculation about Iranian space technology's role in its missile armaments. That speculation did not justify the U.S. program since it was known that Iran already had missiles with a capability of 2,000 km. He then added that,

> Within the framework of its space program, Iran is preparing to launch a satellite to a low-altitude orbit. A rocket has been built for this purpose and it is being tested. The first test was held in February 2008, but, by all accounts, failed to achieve the task set. The current second rocket, according to Iranian mass media, was a success, and a mock-up satellite was put into orbit. If this is confirmed by space control means, Iran has approached the stage of putting a satellite into earth orbit, using its own launch vehicle.[116]

Thus Nesterenko, while denying it, confirmed General Sazhin's forebodings and threat assessment.

Iran's Omid satellite launch of February 2, 2009, also confirmed Sazhin's warnings.[117] As a result of this launch, Vitaly Lopota, President of Russia's Energiya Corporation, stated that Iran now has missiles capable of reaching any spot on earth.[118] Yesin now claims that the fact that,

> Iran has put a satellite with the Safir rocket — an up-graded and re-equipped version of the combat missile Shihab-3M — is evidence that it has at its disposal a medium-range missile, capable of delivering 100-150 kilogram payloads to a destination located 3,500-4,000 kilometers away. If the payload is increased at least to 1,000 kilograms — and this is a payload an interconti-nental ballistic missile should be capable of carrying quite easily — the range of the Iranian missile will in-evitably reduce to 2,200 kilometers.[119]

He also stated that if Iran is assisted by other countries (and we know that it is receiving help from North Korea if not from others — author), then, given the progress its scientists have made, Iran, by 2014, will be able to create its own ICBMs.[120] Similarly, the U.S. Institute for Foreign Policy Assessments reported in late 2008 that,

> Projecting Iran's extant capabilities into the future, and with an eye on how Iran's nuclear force posture might evolve, it is safe to say that Iran is likely to pursue development of a serious long-range ballistic missile capability, supported potentially by satellite guidance technologies, perhaps to attain a limited counterforce capability. Iran already is developing an interconti-nental ballistic missile (ICBM), and it is known to be experimenting with multiple independently targeted re-entry vehicle (MIRV) technologies, using its space-launch program basis for some of this technology de-velopment.[121]

41

And if we look at cruise missiles, against which Russia has highly ineffective defenses, the picture of Iran's developing capabilities is equally sobering.[122] Indeed, the Obama administration has already essentially repudiated the national intelligence estimate of 2007 and has concluded that Iran is unquestionably seeking a nuclear weapon.[123]

Similarly, President Putin's 2007 proposal for joint use of the Gabala air and missile defense installation in Azerbaijan implicitly acknowledged the validity of the U.S. threat perception concerning Iran. As one Iranian newspaper wrote in September 2007,

> Meanwhile, the change of stance by Russia regarding the anti-missile defense shield, from criticizing it and rejecting it to proposing the use of an alternative site for that system, could be regarded as a remarkable development that indicates the serious threats posed by that project. In the case of the implementation of a 'joint missile defense system' and the installation of intercepting radar systems in our neighboring countries—the Republic of Azerbaijan, Turkey, Iraq, or Kuwait—would include the intensification of American threats against our country.[124]

Thus Moscow clearly knows that Iran is building ballistic missiles with a range of 3,500-4,000 km or more that threaten Russia's territory and vital interests, although they argue that it is only building them in the tens, not hundreds, of missiles.[125]

Neither do potential problems end here. In 2009 Russian naval officers were arrested in Kyrgyzstan for trying to sell China restricted anti-ship missiles, suggesting that, as in the case of the *Arctic Sea*, the officer corps has more than a few "entrepreneurs" in it who are willing to sell advanced weapons abroad for money. In another example, i.e., Myanmar, Moscow's penetration of the local arms market was reportedly effected not by the state or Rosoboroneksport (ROE), but by Russia's intelligence agencies, giving rise to questions of whether or not the government has complete control over its arms sales to Myanmar, as those should be conducted by ROE and the MoD.[126] Given Myanmar's inclinations towards developing nuclear energy and its close ties with North Korea, this might not be the soundest policy from the standpoint of advancing Russian national interests.

Given the scope of rogue states' efforts to obtain the weapons and technologies they need or covet, the consequences of this corruption can be dangerous not only in terms of first-order effects, but also in terms of second and third-order effects. Apart from the international consequences of such corrupt transfer of arms to these states, the dangers to Russia are now quite visible. Once again, the personal interests of key government officials and agencies seem to be as much drivers of policy as are allegedly geostrategic and geopolitical considerations. And these personal or sectoral considerations have clearly put Russian interests at some degree of risk either politically in Latin America or, more dangerously, by placing Russia's territory and that of its CIS partners at a not insignificant risk from Iran.

Tandemocracy and Civil-Military Relations.

There can be little doubt that these instances of corruption in the arms sales realm derive, a least in part from the pervasive corruption of the state that is intrinsic to its governance. But the state's political structure also aggravates the many dangers its defective civil-military relations could pose for Russia. The current tandemocracy of Medvedev and Putin offers significant potential dangers in this regard. It represents a wholly manipulated show of legality and democracy masking the legal nihilism designed to overcome the true achilles heel of Russian politics, namely the succession question. But it has failed to do so because it is already clear that the issue of the 2012 presidential election provides a challenge that is almost impossible, if not impossible, to meet by truly democratic and legal means. Evidently both Putin and Medvedev intend, as of now, to compete for the presidency, which will threaten the equilibrium and lead to just that kind of elite cleavage that could undermine this system.[127]

What we already know is that there appears to be, if not a personal rivalry between Medvedev and Putin, then certainly a policy struggle between their respective entourages. But this struggle is one where Putin and his supporters, drawn like him from the Russian power structures (*Silovye Struktury*) especially the old KGB, have apparently prevailed until now. Although there has been a lot of discussion about this rivalry and its domestic policy implications, the potential repercussions for Russia's foreign and domestic policies are also quite serious.

Moreover, Putin clearly feels that, despite the constitution reserving defense issues to the President, he can comment publicly on major defense issues and throw his weight around on them, e.g., his December 29, 2009, comments on the impending nuclear weapon treaty with the United States blaming the U.S. missile defenses for the delay and demanding that Russia build offensive weapons and insist upon the United States linking defenses to offenses or getting rid of its missile defenses.[128] Putin's statements, when compared to Medvedev's anodyne comment that the U.S. and Russian positions on the treaty were close, indicate his desire to upstage Medvedev, show who is boss, and play to the anti-American tendencies so prevalent among many members of the elite. In other words, he is conducting his own security policy.[129] Not only do Putin's statements throw a monkey wrench into the negotiations to conclude the treaty, he also deliberately impeded senatorial ratification of the treaty and, as General (Ret.) Vladimir Dvorkin, one of Russia's leading experts, underscored, sought to maintain the concept of mutual deterrence that presupposes mutual hostility with the United States.[130]

This is by no means his sole obstruction of defense and security policy. A recent article by Mikhail Zygar laid out all the cases of foreign and defense rivalry. The government of Nauru was evidently promised $50 million by Putin's team, not the regular government, to recognize South Ossetia and Abkhazia as independent states. Similarly Russia's in and out again stance on membership in the World Trade Organization (WTO) in 2008-10 owes much to this rivalry, which has obstructed a clear and coherent posture on this issue. Instead, the Putin group tried to impose a customs union, with Belarus and Kazakhstan all entering together under Russian leadership into the WTO. Putin also blocked the implementation of the Northern Dimension transit route to bring supplies to NATO forces in Afghanistan. Thus the bureaucracy, especially the armed forces, is blocking the agreement, and as of the end of 2009, there had been just two such flights. Only afterward did full-scale commitment to this route begin.[131]

Putin had also insisted on dragging out the negotiations on arms control with the United States before his speech, because he apparently wanted to "demonstrate that Obama received the Nobel Prize for nothing" and did not want the United States to chalk up this agreement on offensive weapons to its credit. In private conversations at the time, Russian diplomats, who are powerless to stop Putin, admitted that the treaty might be shelved altogether, and Foreign Minister Lavrov meanwhile charged that the United States has refused to negotiate seriously. In the meantime, governments in the CIS have begun to resist Moscow's pressure as its policies become more demanding and, dare we say, chauvinist.[132]

Indeed the Russian press has recently commented upon the appearance of friction as Medvedev acquires leadership experience and greater international recogniton.[133] The essence of the problem lies in the following situation.

> Russia's policy process is opaque and informal: the highest authority, especially in matters of national security, is theoretically vested in the president. The current incumbent [Dmitri Medvedev] however, appears to play second fiddle to the strongman prime minister [Vladimir Putin], who skillfully balances interests of powerful financial-industrial clans closely connected to the machinery of the Russian state. This political system produces endless intrigue and policy debates, often without an obvious resolution and execution. [134]

This press report cited three examples, but this friction was already apparent in 2008. Once again, Latin American policies are instructive in this context for they show the same thing.

This Latin American example illustrates that the rivalry opens up areas for well-connected political entrepreneurs like Igor Sechin, acting on behalf of Putin, to launch defense and foreign policy initiatives that expose Russia to some risk and dangerous adventures and suggests that the military services are being drawn into this game on one or another contender's side, a further example of politicization of the armed forces and the increasingly risk-accepting behavior of the Russian government. Displaying that strategic motivation to counter U.S. policy, President Putin, even before the Georgian war of 2008, also seemed to be trying to conduct his own security and foreign policy in competition with his heir, President Medvedev, by planting hints among military men that Russia should restore its relations with Cuba and establish an air base there. He even sent Deputy Prime Minister Igor Sechin and Security Council Secretary Nikolai Patrushev to Cuba in 2008 to discuss enhanced cooperation between the two states. Given Patrushev's position as Head of the Security Council, this could only mean defense cooperation. Such moves clearly aimed to irritate the United States gratuitously. Cuba refused to bite because these plans were publicly announced without consulting it in advance, further evidence that they served interests other than that of Cuba.[135] Cuba's Foreign Minister even denied any knowledge of the Russian plan for deploying military sites there, and Fidel Castro publicly praised Raul Castro's restraint in refusing to be provoked by Moscow or by U.S. Air Force Chief of Staff General Norton Schwartz, who said that such a base would be crossing the red line.[136]

But we cannot exclude further developments along that line. Indeed, not only did Sechin promote further economic deals and arms sales to Cuba, Venezuela, and Nicaragua, he also discussed with them the formation of an alliance, as "Moscow considers the formation of such a union a worthy response to U.S. activity in the former Soviet Union and the formerly proposed placement of missile defenses in Poland and the Czech Republic."[137] Not surprisingly, Sechin reported to Putin that Moscow should upgrade its relations with these countries in particular, and Latin America in general.[138] But if such an alliance does actually materialize, then, given its open military component and arms sales, it would pose a serious threat to Latin American and U.S. interests.

In March 2009, it became clear that Moscow factions were still trying to militarize ties to Latin America. Lieutenant General Anatoly Zikharev, Commander in Chief of Russia's Long-Range Aviation, claimed that President Chavez had offered the island of L'Orchila as a temporary base for his forces, i.e., strategic bombers, and that Cuba could also serve such a purpose. Chavez quickly backpedaled, saying that he had only said Russian planes could land there if this fit into Moscow's plans. And Cuba again remained silent. Still there are reports that Cuba has agreed to host a Russian satellite tracking station, which would represent a Russian effort to recover something like what it used to have at Lourdes before 2001.[139] Obviously somebody in Moscow wanted to raise this issue of Latin American bases, and the Air Force and Navy clearly want such bases. But again the government quashed the whole idea, and it has not been raised again.[140] Nevertheless, it appears that Latin American policy is an issue linking Chavez with Russia's "hawks" and *Siloviki* (members and politicians who are alumni of the power structures, police, army, etc.) in the Russian political struggle.

The Russian media reports of significant differences in foreign policy also touch on sensitive defense issues. Whereas Presidents Obama and Medvedev agreed on the framework of an arms control treaty at their July 2009 summit, Russian specialists, apparently designated by Putin, began to insist on taking account of not only U.S. but also United Kingdom (UK) and French nuclear forces. This led Medvedev to try and resolve outstanding issues in the negotiations with Washington more quickly. Second, in regard to China policy, Sechin, rather than Medvedev, appears to be the main Russian foreign policy actor, and he has not only an interest in Putin triumphing, but a personal pecuniary interest as head of the Rosneft oil company in China policy, suggesting that the fusion of personal and political interests at the highest level continues with deleterious effects for Russia regarding its ties with China.

Third, the Ministry of Foreign Affairs, which Putin (against the constitution) supervises, leaned hard on Armenia to make concessions to Turkey in the recent normalization process of 2008-09, making Medvedev very unhappy about his exclusion from an active role in that issue. Evidently what motivated Putin was the desire to obtain Turkey's assent to construction of the proposed South Stream gas pipeline in its territorial waters in the Black Sea. While this objective was attained, it clearly reflected the division between Medvedev and Putin.[141] Thus, this rivalry not only can lead to consequential foreign and defense policies of the utmost significance for Russia: ties with the United States and Latin America, arms control, relations with China, and ties to Turkey; it also fosters the politicization of the armed forces and rather risky efforts at projecting power abroad.

THE NEW DEFENSE LAW

The urge to project power abroad and take a tough line with the United States for its own sake also merges in other ways with the legal nihilism cited above in the new additions to the Law on Defense. For all its talk of adhering to international law, Russia, in fact does not recognize the sovereignty or territorial integrity of the states emerging after 1989 or its eastern European neighbors as being full or immutable. At the NATO-Russia Council in April 2008 in Bucharest, Romania, President Putin told President Bush, "But, George, don't you understand that Ukraine is not a state?" Putin further claimed that most of its territory was a Russian gift in the 1950s. Moreover, while Western Ukraine belonged to Eastern Europe, Eastern Ukraine was "ours." Furthermore, if Ukraine did enter NATO, Russia would then dismember Ukraine and graft its parts onto Russia, and thus Ukraine would cease to exist as a state.[142] Putin also said that Russia regards NATO enlargement as a threat, so if Georgia received membership, Moscow would "take adequate measures" and recognize Abkhazia and South Ossetia to create a buffer between NATO and Russia.[143] As we have seen since then, these were not idle threats.

Since then Medvedev has called upon the Duma to pass a new law amending the previous Law on Defense, which it subsequently has done and which he recently signed into law. Specifically he urged it to revise the existing laws to pass a new law,

> The draft law would supplement Clause 10 of the Federal Law on Defense with paragraph 21 specifying that in line with the generally accepted principles and pro-

visions of international law, the Russian Federation's international treaties, and the Federal Law on Defense; Russian Armed Forces can be used in operations beyond Russia's borders for the following purposes:

- To counter an attack against Russian Armed Forces or other troops deployed beyond Russia's borders;

- To counter or prevent an aggression against another country;

- To protect Russian citizens abroad;

- To combat piracy and ensure safe passage of shipping.

The draft suggests that the Federal Law on Defence be supplemented with Clause 101, setting, in accordance with Russia's Constitution, the procedures for decisions on use of Russian Armed Forces beyond the country's borders.[144]

Not only would this law provide a "legal" basis for the offensive projection of Russian military force beyond Russia's borders, it would thus justify the war of 2008 and any subsequent attack against Georgia in response to alleged attacks on "the Russian citizens" of the supposedly independent states of Abkhazia and South Ossetia. It also provides a basis for justifying the offensive use of Russian force against every state from the Baltic to Central Asia on the self-same basis of supposedly defending the "honor and dignity" of Russian citizens and culture from discrimination and attack. This whole episode also tells us that Medvedev's instruction to the Duma indicated his awareness, even if it remained implicit, that the war with Georgia was illegal under Russian law at the time. This should not surprise us. After all, in the wake of the Russo-Geor-gian war, Medvedev announced that he would form his foreign policy on five principles. Among them are principles that give Russia a license for intervening in other states where the Russian minority's "interests and dignity" are allegedly at risk. Medvedev also as-serted that Russia has privileged interests with coun-tries which he would not define, demonstrating that Russia not only wants to revise borders or intervene in other countries, it also demands a sphere of influence in Eurasia as a whole.[145] Here again, we see that legal nihilism is directly linked to the threat of politicized military action abroad on the flimsiest of bases.

In many respects the language of this new law con-tradicts international law and the UN's language per-taining to relevant situations. As one Russian source told the newspaper *Kommersant*, the president has re-ceived what amounts to "general power of attorney independently to decide issues of the Russian mili-tary's participation in operations outside Russia."[146]

Beyond that,

> Due to its vague and ambiguous wording, the new Russian legislation has radically expanded the range of circumstances under which Moscow considers it legitimate to deploy troops abroad, as well as the list of states in which Russia may station armed forces in accordance with the law.[147]

Second,

> The clause concerning the protection of Russian citi-zens in foreign states grants Moscow the right of uni-lateral military intrusion into any country in which Russian citizens reside on a permanent or temporary basis under a wide set of arbitrarily construed circum-

stances. It does not specify precisely what 'an armed attack' constitutes, how many Russian citizens need to be under attack to justify Russian intervention, whether such an attack would be carried out by armed forces or law-enforcement agencies of a foreign state or by non-state armed groups, and whether the Russian government has to obtain an official sanction to act in a foreign territory from the UN Security Council or from the authorities of the particular state where Russian citizens are under attack. [148]

Third, this law radically alters the security situation in the CIS because it gives Russia a legal platform, so to speak, for justifying its unilateral intervention into any of the other members' territory that is not provided for in the founding documents of existing treaty organizations in the CIS and thus undermines their validity and with it the protection of those other states' sovereignty and integrity. As Yuri Fedorov writes,

Russia's self-proclaimed right to defend its troops against armed attacks affects Moscow's relations with Armenia, Belarus, Kazakhstan, Kyrgyzstan, Tajikistan and Uzbekistan, all of which are parties to the Collective Security Treaty Organization [CSTO] and, with the exception of Belarus, the Shanghai Cooperation Organization [SCO], and which also have bilateral arrangements on military assistance with Russia. Russian troops and military facilities are deployed in all of these states, with the exception of Uzbekistan. Neither the Collective Security Treaty, nor any bilateral arrangements imply Russia's right to make unilateral decisions about the form, scope and very fact of employing its forces in the aforementioned states. All of these issues were to be decided either by all parties to the CSTO collectively, or by parties to the corresponding bilateral treaty. Decisions on counter-terrorist activities in the framework of the SCO are made by consensus. The new Russian legislation did not cancel out the multilateral or bilateral decision-making procedures yet it devalued those procedures in a sense. If Russian troops deployed in some of these countries are involved in international or internal conflicts, which is quite possible, Moscow will have a pretext for using them and duly deploying additional units in a unilateral manner. The right to defend Russian troops on foreign soil is of particular importance for Russia's relations with Ukraine and Moldova. The Ukrainian government has demanded the withdrawal of the Russian naval base after 2017, while Moldova insists on the immediate departure of Russian troops from Transdniestria. In turn, Moscow has set its sights on stationing its troops there indefinitely. In such a context, skirmishes of any degree of gravity involving Russian servicemen in these countries may furnish Moscow with a pretext for military intervention.[149]

Fourth, as Fedorov notes, this law directly contradicts the language of the draft treaty on European security submitted by Medvedev to European governments on November 29, 2009.[150] While that draft treaty preaches multilateralism, the new law shows that, "Moscow favors a unilateral approach towards security issues and wants a free hand if and when conflict situations arise."[151] Fifth, Medvedev wants to free himself from any constraint of consultation with legislative bodies over this decision. When the law was passed in November 2009, he had to agree to a proviso in the law that he had to consult with the Federation Council on the question of dispatching troops abroad in these circumstances. But by December, he was demanding unfettered power to make this decision unilaterally. In other words, we are coming to a point where a president may send troops abroad for the vaguest of pretexts without any accountability whatsoever. Legal nihilism only begins to describe this situation. [152] Or, as Felgenhauer observes, this law represents a constitutional coup.[153]

Finally and sixth, as Fedorov observes, this law may also shed some light on Moscow's thinking about future power projection scenarios beyond its borders. Specifically,

> In particular, the Russian intelligence services may plan to ignite disturbances and ethnic clashes in Sevastopol, resulting in attacks against the Black Sea Fleet servicemen or facilities by criminal groups or an unruly mob. This would give Russia the legal grounds to intervene militarily in the Crimean peninsula, occupy Sevastopol or the whole peninsula and retain its naval base for an indefinite period of time. Another scenario presupposes the engineering of ethnic clashes in Estonia and/or Latvia, which may be exploited by Moscow as a pretext for military intervention, or at least for the threat of such intervention. Widespread rioting and looting in Tallinn in April 2007, provoked by the decision to relocate the Soviet Army monument, yet fuelled and orchestrated by Russian agents, confirmed that Moscow has enough instruments at its disposal to destabilize the situation in large cities in Latvia and Estonia with a substantial proportion of ethnic Russians.[154]

Where the president has unchallenged power to deploy forces at home or abroad the politicization of the security sector in a condition of tandemocracy or dual power (*Dvoevlastie* in Russian) is fraught with danger for both foreign and domestic policy. Although the Putin era supposedly represented an era of heightened control over policy, it is entirely plausible to argue that in fact the fissiparous tendencies that were so observable under Yeltsin have continued and continue to challenge central policymakers.[155] But under conditions of this dual power these conflicts, some of which we have already cited, have now openly emerged in the security sector.

For example, the importance of the Ministry of Interior and its forces (MVD and VVMVD) to the state are incontestable. In fact, until relatively recently, the bulk of spending on security went to them rather than the armed forces, reflecting the government's awareness that the primary threats were within, not external to Russia.[156] However, the MVD is known to be an extremely corrupt institution whose defects have been seized upon in the recent scandal of the death of the 37-year-old lawyer of Hermitage Capital, Sergei Magnitsky, in prison. This scandal has even led to calls for a purge or even liquidation of the ministry in order to reform it.[157] But behind the calls for a purge or even liquidation of the ministry stand those members of Medvedev's entourage, allegedly led by Vladislav Surkov, who seek to use this incident to break down the MVD, which has been a stronghold of the Putin faction and the *Siloviki*. Although they have had limited success in forcing dismissals of some officials there for this scandal and other examples of malfeasance, like the explosion of an ammunition dump in Ulyanovsk, in fact, they have not yet successfully forced the wholesale purging of the MVD because, as Alexander Golts wrote, the President cannot dismiss the Minister, Rashid Nurglaiev, because he is not in the president's nomenklatura, the list of officials over whom the president has power.[158] Clearly, this attempt to further politicize the MVD is fraught with extraordinarily dangerous potential consequences, for such games may go on to embrace the army on critical foreign policy questions as we have already seen. And the army's politicization, as we also know, has long since been approved from above.[159]

CONCLUSIONS

As Barany and Gomart, among others, have observed, civil-military issues and relations are not a technical question but go to the heart of Russia's domestic and foreign policy projects.[160] The anti-democratic nature of those relations and the reliance of both sides of this dyad on the incessant invocation of foreign threats contribute in many ways to the fact that Russia, as such, intrinsically remains a risk factor and is so acknowledged by Russian analysts. Two last points here are particularly relevant. First, Russia's numerous pathologies in the area of civil-military relationship highlights the fact that the principles of constructing the security sector under democratic conditions give rise to security and peace among states, but that failure to do so breeds endemic, enduring, and structural insecurity within states (in this case Russia) and among their neighbors.[161]

Second, all the cases presented above point to the fact that not only is Medvedev and his team unable to control the discussion over the nature of threats to Russia and the appropriate responses to them, but that he clearly has imperfect control over the state and overall security sector (i.e., the *Silovye Struktury*). Under conditions of the tandemocracy and the phenomena listed above, these facts again bring home to us the fact that the intrinsic nature of Russia's governmental structure is the reason why it remains a perennial risk factor in international security.[162]

The persistence of an archaic, even neo-feudal, structure of power that fuses power and property under a political structure reminiscent of late Tsarism is itself impressive testimony to Russia's fundamental instability, a fact that its leaders have also always grasped. Yeltsin and Putin's regressive steps to institutionalize this system have paradoxically contributed to a situation where the President directly confronts his military institutions without benefit of a public body to enforce accountability, transparency, and depoliticization.[163] This does not mean a coup is imminent, or even likely; indeed, neither alternative is foreseeable anytime soon. Nor does it mean that war is around the corner. But it does mean that both wars and coups (whether by generals or by politicians leading generals) remain ever present possibilities in Russia. Consequently and owing in considerable measure to the system that has emerged, neither is Russia's true security or that of its neighbors foreseeable anytime soon. And that problem is an enduring one that will not change until and unless Russia changes.

ENDNOTES - CHAPTER 1

1. Thomas Gomart, *Russian Civil-Military Relations: Putin's Legacy,* Washington, DC: Carnegie Endowment for International Peace, 2008, p. 87.

2. Zoltan Barany, *Democratic Breakdown and the Decline of the Russian Military,* Princeton, NJ: Princeton University Press, 2007, p. 177.

3. Dale R. Herspring, "Is Military Reform in Russia for 'Real'? Yes, But," Stephen Blank and Richard Weitz, eds., *The Russian Military Today and Tomorrow,* Carlisle, PA: Strategic Studies Institute, U.S. Army War College, 2010; Stephen Blank, "'No Need To Threaten Us, We Are Frightened of Ourselves,' Russia's Blueprint

for a Police State, The New Security Strategy," Blank and Weitz, eds.

4. *Ibid.*; Moscow, *Interfax*, in Russian, November 18, 2009, *Open Source Center* Central Eurasia, *Foreign Broadcast Information Service* (Henceforth *FBIS SOV*), November 18, 2008.

5. Pavel Felgenhauer, "Russia's Imperial General Staff," *Perspective*, Vol. XVI, No. 1, October-November, 2005, available from *www.bu.ed./iscip/vol16/felgenhauer*.

6. "Putin Interviewed by Journalists from G8 countries — text," June 4, 2007, available from *www.kremlin.ru*; Moscow, *Agentstvo Voyennykh Novostey Internet Version*, in English, May 16, 2007, *Open Source Committee, FBIS SOV*, May 16, 2007.

7. Andrei Illarionov, "The Siloviki in Charge," *Journal of Democracy*, Vol. XX, No. 2, April, 2009, p. 72.

8. Leon Aron, "The Problematic Pages," *The New Republic*, September 24, 2008, pp. 35-40; Stephen Blank, "Web War I: Is Europe's First Information War a New Kind of War?" *Comparative Strategy*, Vol. XXVII, No. 3, 2008, pp. 227-247.

9. Brian Whitmore, "Did Russia Plan Its War in Georgia?" *Radio Free Europe Radio Liberty*, August 15, 2008; Pavel Felgenhauer, "Moscow Ready For Major Confrontations With Pro-Western Georgia and Ukraine," both from *Eurasia Daily Monitor*, June 19, 2008; Pavel Felgenhauer, "Eta Byla Ne Spontannaya a Splanirovannaya Voina" ("It was not a spontaneous but rather a preplanned ewar"), *Novaya Gazeta*, August 14, 2008, available from *www.novayagazeta.ru/data/2008/59/04.html*; James Traub, "Taunting the Bear," *New York Times*, August 11, 2008, available from *www.nytimes.com*; Dov Lynch, *Engaging Eurasia's Separatist States: Unresolved Conflicts and De Facto States*, Washington, DC: United States Institute of Peace Press, 2004, p. 57; Vladimir Frolov, "Russia Profile Weekly Experts Panel: Russia going To War With Georgia," available from *www.russiaprofile.com*; "Georgia: A Fresh Outbreak of Violence During Negotiations," August 7, 2008, available from *www.stratfor.com*; "Geopolitical Diary, Decision Time in South Ossetia," August 8, 2008, available from *www.stratfor.com*; Vladimir Socor, "Berlin Consultations on Abkhazia Derailed," *Eurasia Dai-*

ly Monitor, August 1, 2008; Vladimir Socor, "Ossetian Separatists Are Provoking a Major Russian Intervention," *Eurasia Daily Monitor*, August 7, 2008; Boris Dolgin, "Military Continuation: What Is Happening Around South Ossetia," Moscow, *FBIS SOV*, August 8, 2008, available from *Polit.ru Internet Version*; Vadim Dubnov, "Who Fired the First Shot," Moscow, Gazeta, in Russian, August 6, 2008, *FBIS* SOV, August 6, 2008; Moscow, *Interfax*, in Russia, August 6, 2008, *FBIS SOV*, August 6, 2008; Yevgeny Shestakov, "From South to North Evacuation of Children From South Ossetia Continues," Moscow, *Rossiyskaya Gazeta*, in Russian, August 5, 2008, *FBIS SOV* August 5, 2008; "Talking Through Gritted Teeth," *BBC Monitoring*, August 6, 2008; Yuliya Latynina, "South Ossetia Crisis Could Be Russia's Chance To Defeat Siloviki," *Radio Free Europe Radio Liberty*, August 8, 2008; Georgi Lomsadze, "Georgia Tensions Flare Over Breakaway South Ossetia, *Eurasia Insight*, August 4, 2008; "Who's To Blame In South Ossetia," *Radio Free Europe Radio Liberty*, August 8, 2008.

10. Timofei Bordachev, "Russia's Europe Dilemma: Democratic Partner vs. Authoritarian Satellite," Andrew Kuchins and Dmitri Trenin, eds., *Russia: The Next Ten Years, A Collection of Essays to Mark Ten Years of the Carnegie Moscow Center*, Moscow, Russia: Carnegie Center, 2004, p. 120.

11. Barany.

12. "Memorandum From Martin McAuley," House of Commons Defence Committee, *Russia: A New Confrontation? Team Report of Session 2008-09*, London, UK: The Stationery House for the House of Commons, 2009, p. EV 76.

13. Vladimir Shlapentokh, "Putin as a Perfect Politician, *Johnson's Russia List*, December 18, 2009, available from *shlapentokh.wordpress.com*.

14. *Ibid.*, pp. 76-98.

15. Pavel Felgenhauer, "Russian Security Council Plans to Draft Military Doctrine," *Eurasia Daily Monitor*, March 22, 2007.

16. Barany, pp. 167-168.

17. *Ibid.*

18. *Ibid.;* Alexander Mikhailov, p. 2.

19. "Russia On the Brink of Civil War," Moscow, *Vlasti*, in Russian, April 19, 2009, *FBIS SOV*, April 19, 2009.

20. *Ibid.*

21. *Ibid.*

22. Iriana Borogan, "In Shoulder-Boards: The Kremlin's Anti-Crisis Project: When OMON Rushes to Help," Moscow, *Yezhenedevnyi Zhurnal*, in Russian, December 15, 2009, *FBIS SOV*, December 15, 2009.

23. Moscow, *Agentstvo Voyennykh Novostey Internet Version*, in Russian, July 4, 2008, *FBIS SOV*, July 4, 2008.

24. McAuley, p. EV 98.

25. Stephen Blank, "Map Reading: NATO's and Russia's Pathways to European Military Integration," Occasional Papers of the Woodrow Wilson Center, No. 61, February 2001, also published in *Review of International Affairs*, Vol. I, No. 1, pp. 31-52, 2001.

26. See for example, Stephen Blank, "The Putin Succession and Its Implications for Russian Politics," *Post-Soviet Affairs*, Vol. XXIV, No. 3, September, 2008, pp. 231-262.

27. Madrid ABC.es, in Spanish, July 3, 2008, *FBIS SOV*, July 3, 2008.

28. Anatoly S. Kulikov, "Organized Crime in Russia: Domestic Developments and International Implications," Yuri Fedorov and Bertil Nygren, eds., *Russia and Europe: Putin's foreign Policy*, Stockholm, Sweden: Swedish National Defense College, 2005, pp. 115-128.

29. "Defense Ministry Will Shed Excess Equipment," RFE/RL Newsline, April 3, 2008, available from *www.rferl.org/content/Article/1144084.html*. See also "Russian Official Says 30 Percent of Military Budget Lost Through Corruption," *Agentstvo Voyennykh*

Novostey, July 2, 2008, also in *World New Connection* (hereafter WNC) (articles available by subscription from *wnc.fedworld.gov/index.html*).

30. Moscow, *RIA OREANDA,* in Russian, July 1, 2009, *FBIS SOV* August 17, 2009.

31. Remarks by Stephen Blank, Eugene Rumer, Mikhail Tsypkin, and Alexander Golts at the Heritage Foundation Program, "The Russian Military: Modernization and the Future," April 8, 2008, available from *www.heritage.org/press/events/ev040808a.cfm.*

32. Moscow, *RIA Novosti,* in Russian, August 31, 2009, *FBIS SOV,* August 31, 2009.

33. Moscow, *Vechernyaa Moskva,* in Russian, August 31, 2009, *FBIS SOV,* August 31, 2009.

34. Yuri Gavrilov, "Robbery to Order," Moscow, *Rossiyskaya Gazeta,* in Russian June 17, 2009, *FBIS SOV,* June 17, 2009.

35. Moscow, *ITAR-TASS,* in Russian, September 23, 2009, *FBIS SOV,* September 23, 2009.

36. Moscow, *Vesti TV,* in Russian, August 30, 2009, *Open Source Center, FBIS SOV,* August 30, 2009.

37. "Crime Rate In Russian Military Rises 9% in 2008," *RIA Novosti,* March 26, 2009.

38. "Interview With Lieutenant General A. S. Surochkin, Deputy Chairman of the Investigations Committee Attached to Russian Federation Prosecutor's office and Head of the Military Investigations Directorate, by Aleksandr' Kots, Moscow, *Komsomolskaya Pravda,* in Russian, September 7, 2009, *FBIS SOV,* September 7, 2009.

39. *Ibid.*

40. "Crime Among Russian Military Officers Highest in Decade," *RIA Novosti,* July 9, 2009.

41. *Ibid.*; "Crime Soars to 10-Year High in Army," *Moscow Times,* July 10, 2009.

42. William Jackson, "Russian Military, Organized Crime In On Cyberattacks Against Georgia," *Government Computer News*, August 17, 2009.

43. Moscow, *Vesti TV*, in Russian, July 27, 2009, available from *Gazeta.ru*, *FBIS SOV*, July 27, 2009; author's conversations with members of European foreign ministries and intelligence services, 2008; Keith C. Smith, *Russian Energy Politics in the Baltics, Poland, and the Ukraine: A New Stealth Imperialism?*, Washington, DC: Center for Strategic and International Studies, 2004; Anita Orban, *Power, Energy, and the New Russian Imperialism*, Washington, DC: Praeger, 2008; Edward Lucas, *The New Cold War: Putin's Russia and the Threat to the West*, London, UK: Palgrave Macmillan, 2008; Robert Larsson, *Nord Stream, Sweden and Baltic Sea Security*, Stockholm, Sweden: Swedish Defense Research Agency, 2007; Robert Larsson; *Russia´s Energy Policy: Security Dimensions and Russia´s Reliability as an Energy Supplier*, Stockholm, Sweden: Swedish Defense Research Agency, 2006; Janusz, Bugajski *Cold Peace: Russia's New Imperialism*: Washington, DC: Center for Strategic and International Studies, Praeger, 2004; Richard Krickus, *Iron Troikas,* Carlisle, PA: Strategic Studies Institute, U.S. Army War College, 2006; Valery Ratchev, "Bulgaria and the Future of European Security," paper presented to the SSI-ROA Conference, "Eurasian Security in the Era of NATO Enlargement," Prague, Czech Republic, August 4-5, 1997; Laszlo Valki, "Hungary and the Future of European Security," *Ibid.*; Stefan Pavlov, "Bulgaria in a Vise," *Bulletin of the Atomic Scientists*, January-February 1998, pp. 28-31; Moscow, *Izvestiya*, in Russian, June 19, 1997, in *FBIS SOV*, pp. 97-169, June 18, 1997; Sofia, Bulgaria, *Novinar*, in Bulgarian, April 10, 1998, in *Foreign Broadcast Information Service, Eastern Europe* (*FBIS EEU*), pp. 98-100, April 13, 1998.

44. Author's conversations with European foreign ministry and intelligence officials, 2008.

45. "Courts Take Unduly Soft Line Toward Police Violence-Media," *ITAR-TASS*, August 17, 2009.

46. Vitaly Shlykov, "The Economics of Defense in Russia and the Legacy of Structural Militarization," in Steven E. Miller and Dmitri Trenin, eds., *The Russian Military: Power and Purpose*, Cambridge, MA: MIT Press, 2004., pp. 160-182; Vitaly Shlykov, "The Anti-Oligarchy Campaign and its Implications for Russia's Security," *European Security*, Vol. XVII, No. 2, 2004, pp. 11-128; Leonid Kosals, "Criminal Influence/Criminal Control Over the Russian Military-Industrial Complex in the Context of Global Security," *NATO Defense College Research Paper*, No. 1, March, 2004, pp. 6-8; "Moscow, *Ekho Moskvy*, in Russian, June 4, 2004, *FBIS SOV*, June 4, 2004, *Moscow, ITAR-TASS*, April 14, 2005, *FBIS SOV*, April 14, 2005; *Moscow Center TV*, in Russian, September 30, 2003; *FBIS SOV*, October 1, 2003; Moscow, *Moskovskaya Pravda*, in Russian, April 17, 2003, *FBIS SOV*, April 17, 2003; Moscow, "Interview With OAO *Gipromez* General director Vitaly Rogozhin, *Rossiyskaya Gazeta*, in Russian, July 13, 2005, *FBIS SOV*, July 13, 2005; Janusz Bugajski, *Cold Peace: Russia's New Imperialism*, Washington, DC, and Westport, CT: Praeger Publishers, 2005; Richard J. Krickus, "The Presidential Crisis in Lithuania: Its Roots and the Russian Factor," Remarks at the Woodrow Wilson Center, Washington, DC, January 28, 2004 (provided by permission of Dr. Krickus); Krickus, *Iron Troikas*; Keith C. Smith, *Russian Energy Politics in the Baltics, Poland, and the Ukraine: A New Stealth Imperialism?* Washington, DC: Center for Strategic and International Studies, 2004; Tor Bukevoll, "Putin's Strategic Partnership With the West: the Domestic Politics of Russian Foreign Policy, *Comparative Strategy*, Vol. XXII, No. 3, 2003, pp. 231-233; Stefan Pavlov, "Bulgaria in a Vise," *The Bulletin of the Atomic Scientists*, January-February, 1998, p. 30; Robert D. Kaplan, "Hoods Against Democrats," *Atlantic Monthly*, December, 1998, pp. 32-36. As Foreign Minister Igor Ivanov said, "Fuel and energy industries in the Balkans are totally dependent on Russia. They have no alternative." "Ivanov on Foreign Policy's Evolution, Goals," *Current Digest of the Post-Soviet Press* (CDPP), Vol. L, No. 43, November 25, 1998, p. 13; U.S.-Slovakia Action Commission: Security and Foreign Policy Working Group, Washington, DC: Center for Strategic and International Studies; and Slovak Foreign Policy Association, *Slovakia's Security and Foreign Policy Strategy*, 2001, Czech Security Information Service, *Annual Report 2000*.

47. Janusz Bugajski, *Back to the Front: Russian Interests in the New Eastern Europe*, Donald Treadgold Papers, No. 41, Seattle, WA: University of Washington Press, 2004, p. 25.

48. Keith C. Smith, *Russian Energy Politics in the Baltics, Poland, and the Ukraine: A New Stealth Imperialism?* Washington, DC: Center for Strategic and International Studies, 2004; Author's conversations with members of European foreign ministries and intelligence services, 2008; Anita Orban, *Power, Energy, and the New Russian Imperialism*, Washington, DC: Praeger, 2008; Lucas, *The New Cold War*; Larsson, *Nord Stream, Sweden and Baltic Sea Security*; Larsson; *Russia´s Energy Policy*; Bugajski, *Cold Peace*; Krickus, *Iron Troikas*; Ratchev, "Bulgaria and the Future of European Security"; Laszlo Valki, "Hungary and the Future of European Security"; *Ibid*; Stefan Pavlov, "Bulgaria in a Vise," *Bulletin of the Atomic Scientists*, January-February 1998, pp. 28-31; Moscow, *Izvestiya*, in Russian, June 19, 1997, in *FBIS SOV*, pp. 97-169, June 18, 1997; Sofia, Bulgaria, *Novinar*.

49. Anton Orekh, "Famine," Moscow, *Yezhenedevnyi Zhurnal Internet Version*, in Russian, July 29, 2008, *FBIS SOV*, July 29, 2008.

50. Dmitri K. Simes and Paul J. Saunders, "The Kremlin Begs To Differ," *The National Interest*, No. 104, November-December, 2009, p. 39.

51. *Ibid.,* pp. 38-42; Ivan Krastev, Mark Leonard and Andrew Wilson, eds., *What Does Russia Think?*, European Council on Foreign Relations, 2009, pp. 1-52, available from *www.ecfr.eu.*

52. Vyacheslav Glazychev, "The "Putin Consensus" Explained, *Ibid.,* p. 13.

53. Roger N. McDermott, "Crisis Looms In Russia's Armed Forces," *Asia Times*, September 4, 2009.

54. *Ibid.*

55. *Ibid.*

56. Pavel Felgenhauer, "Russia's Radical Military Reform in Progress," *Eurasia Daily Monitor*, November 20, 2008.

57. See Don M. Snider, Paul Oh, and Kevin Toner, *The Army's Professional Military Ethic in an Era of Persistent Conflict*, Carlisle, PA: Strategic Studies Institute, U.S. Army War College, 2009, p. 2.

58. Marc Galeotti,"Have Russia's Dirty Generals turned on Shamanov?" *Radio Free Europe Radio Liberty*, September 29, 2009.

59. *Ibid.*

60. "Military Honor is Being Disbanded," *Moskovskiy Komsomolets*, July 30, 2009, available from *www.mk.ru/*; also in WNC, August 1, 2009.

61. "Crime Rates in Army Highest Over Past Ten Years—Prosecutor," *ITAR-TASS*, July 9, 2009; also in WNC, July 10, 2009.

62. Gordon M. Hahn, *Russia's Islamic Threat*, New Haven, CT, and London, UK: Yale University Press, 2007.

63. Aleksandr' Stepanov, "Mountain Law," Moscow, *Nasha Versiya*, in Russian, August 31, 2009, *FBIS SOV*, August 31, 2009.

64. *Ibid.*

65. Mark Franchetti, "Russian Death Squads 'Pulverize' Chechens," *The Times Online*, April 26, 2009, available from *www.timesonline.co.uk.*

66. "Russia Running Death Squads in the Caucasus," *The News,* September 3, 2009, available from *www.thenews.com.pk.*

67. *Ibid.*

68. "Russia Running 'Death Squads' in Caucasus: Rights Groups," *The Dawn*, September 3, 2009, available from *www.dawn.com.*

69. Pavel Felgenhauer, "Military Reform Raises the Specter of a Coup," *Eurasia Daily Monitor*, September 24, 2009; Roman Anin, "The General and Glyba: Why did General Shamanov Send Two Airborne Troops Spetsnaz Teams to Detain an Investigator for Particularly Important Cases?" Moscow, *Novaya Gazeta Online*, in Russian, September 21, 2009, *FBIS SOV*, September 22, 2009.

70. *Ibid.*

71. *Ibid.*

72. Galeotti.

73. Felgenhauer, "Military Reform Raises the Specter of a Coup."

74. In regard to the politicization of the armed forces, see Zoltan Barany, *Democratic Breakdown and the Decline of the Russian Military*, Princeton, NJ: Princeton University Press, 2007.

75. "Two-Thirds of Russian Banks Involved in Money Laundering," *Vremya*, May 23, 2006, available from *pravda.ru, Johnson's Russia List*, May 23, 2006.

76. "Chopping At Tails," May 22, 2006, available from *Gazeta. ru, Johnson's Russia List,* May 23, 2006.

77. Igor Korotchenko, "FSB Takes Defense Complex Under Its Control," Moscow, *Nezavisimaya Gazeta*, in Russian, July 9, 2003, *FBIS SOV*, July 9, 2003.

78. Vitaly Shlykov, "The Economics of Defense in Russia and the Legacy of Structural Militarization," in Miller and Trenin, eds., *The Russian Military*, pp. 160-182; Vitaly Shlykov, "The Anti-Oligarchy Campaign and its Implications for Russia's Security," *European Security*, Vol. XVII, No. 2, 2004, pp. 11-128; Leonid Kosals, "Criminal Influence/Criminal Control Over the Russian Military-Industrial Complex in the Context of Global Security," *NATO Defense College Research Paper*, No. 1, March, 2004, pp. 6-8; *Moscow, Ekho Moskvy in Russian*, June 4, 2004, *FBIS SOV*, June 4, 2004, *Moscow, ITAR-TASS*, April 14, 2005, *FBIS SOV* April 14, 2005; *Moscow Center TV* in Russian, September 30, 2003; *FBIS SOV*, October 1, 2003; Moscow, *Moskovskaya Pravda*, in Russian, April 17, 2003, FBIS SOV, April 17, 2003; Moscow, "Interview With OAO Gipromez General director Vitaly Rogozhin, *Rossiyskaya Gazeta,* in Russian, July 13, 2005, *FBIS SOV*, July 13, 2005.

79. Andrew McGregor, "Concerns Mount Over Hezbollah's Rearmament," *Jamestown Terrorism Focus*, Vol. III, No. 38, October 3, 2006; Iason Athanasiadis, "How Hi-Tech Hezbollah Called the

Shots," *Asia Times Online*, September 9, 2006; Mikhail Barabanov, "Russian Anti-Armor Weapons and Israeli Tanks in Lebanon," *Moscow Defense Brief*, No. 4 (10) 2007, "Russia Denies Supplying Hezbollah with Missiles," *Radio Free Europe Radio Liberty Features*, August 25, 2006.

80. Moscow, *Kommersant in Russian,* July 19, 2000, *FBIS SOV*, July 19, 2000.

81. Moscow, *ITAR-TASS*, in Russian, September 30, 2009, *FBIS SOV*, September 30, 2009.

82. Brian Wood, "International Initiatives To Prevent Illicit Brokering of Arms and Related Materials," *Disarmament Forum*, United Nations Institute for Disarmament Research (UNIDIR), No. 3, 2009, pp. 5-12.

83. Stephen Blank, "Russia in Latin America: Geopolitical Games in the US' Neighborhood," *IFRI Paper,* Russie.Nei.Visions, No. 38, 2009.

84. Tim Johnson and Catherine Belton, "Ex-Soviet Officer Escapes US Extradition," *Financial Times*, August 11, 2009.

85. *Ibid.*

86. An Vranckx, "Arms Brokering Control in the Americas," *Disarmament Forum*, United Nations Institute for Disarmament Research (UNIDIR), No. 3, 2009, p. 31.

87. Moscow, *Kommersant.com*, in English, December 5, 2006, *FBIS SOV*, December 5, 2006; Andy Webb-Vidal, "Cocaine Coasts-Venezuela and West Africa's Drugs Axis," *Jane's Intelligence Review*, January 14, 2009, available from *jir.janes.com/subscribe/jir/doc*; Chris Kraul and Sebastian Rotella, "Venezuela Worries U.S. Counter-Narcotics Officials," *Los Angeles Times*, March 21, 2007, available from *www.latimes.com*; Nicholas Kralev, "Chavez Accused of Ties To Terrorists, " *Washington times*, May 17, 2006, p. 1.

88. Susana Hayward, "Russian Mafia Worms Way into Mexican Drug Cartels," *Miami Herald*, August 11, 2003, *Johnson's Russia List*, August 11, 2003.

89. Available from *www.stratfor.com/analysis/20090202_mexi-co_security_memo_feb_2_2009*; Open Source Center, *OSC Summary*, in Spanish, January 28, 2009, *FBIS SOV*, January 28, 2009.

90. Pavel Sergeyev, "Latin American Maneuvers: Russian Ships Hasten to Visit the Caribbean Region Right After the White Swans," Moscow, in Russian, September 23, 2008, available from *www.Lenta.ru, FBIS SOV*, September 23, 2008.

91. Douglas MacKinnon, "Is Venezuela Going Nuclear?" *Houston Chronicle*, May 27, 2005, available from *ebird.afis.osd.mileb-files/e20050522369795.html*; "Venezuela Aids Iranian Missile Sales to Syria, Intelligence Agencies Say," *Global Security Newswire*, available from *www.nti.org*, December 22, 2008, Moscow, *ITAR-TASS*, in English, November 17, 2008, FBIS *SOV*, November 17, 2008; "Chavez Secures Nuclear, Arms Promises During Russia Visit," *Radio Fee Europe Radio Liberty*, September 26, 2008.

92. "Venezuela's Chavez Says Iran Aiding Uranium Explora-tion," *Radio Free Europe Radio Liberty*, October 18, 2009.

93. Shahram Javadi, "From Backyard to Frontline," Tehran, Iran: *Khorshid*, in Persian December 15, 2008, *FBIS SOV*, December 15, 2008; "Increasing Iranian Presence in Latin America Under-lines Weakening U.S. Position," *Strategic Warning Issues Review*, No. 7, April 2007.

94. "'Israel Link' in Arctic Sea Case," *BBC*, September 9, 2009, available from *news.bbc.co.uk/2/h/europe/8247273.htm*.

95. Vitaly Portnikov, "The Phantom Ship and a Living Mafia," Tel Aviv, *Vesti-2 Supplement*, in Russian, September 10, 2009, *FBIS SOV*, September 10, 2009.

96. "Global Alternative: The Logical Conclusion of a Major Failure of Russian Intelligence," Moscow, in Russian, November 9, 2009, available from *www.forum.msk.ru*, *FBIS SOV*, November 9, 2009.

97. Jerusalem, *DEBKA-Net Weekly Internet Version*, in English, July 21, 2006, *FBIS SOV*, July 21, 2006.

98. Cohen, "Russia and the Axis of Evil: Money, Ambition, and U.S. Interests"; Eugene B. Rumer, "Russia's Policies Toward the Axis of Evil: Money and Geopolitics in Iraq and Iran," Testimony to the House International Relations Committee, February 26, 2003, available from *wwc.house.gov/international_relations/108/ rume0226*; Celeste A. Wallander, "Russian Interest in Trading With the "Axis of Evil," *Ibid.*, available from *wwc.house.internatonal_relations/108/wall/0226.*

99. David Harrison, "Revealed: Russia Spied on Blair for Saddam," *The Daily Telegraph,* April 13, 2003, available from *www.telegraph.co.uk.*

100. Alexander Nemets and Steffany Trofino, "Russia: Tipping the Balance in the Middle East," *Journal of Slavic Military Studies*, Vol. XXII, No. 3, July, 2009, pp. 367-382; Alexander Nemets and Robert W. Kurz, "The Iranian Space Program and Russian Assistance," *Journal of Slavic Military Studies*, vol. XXII, No. 1, 2009, pp. 87-96.

101. Moscow, *Novaya Gazeta Ponedelnik*, in Russian, March 16-22, 1998, *Foreign Broadcast Information Service, Arms Control, (FBIS TAC)* 98-076, March 17, 1998.

102. Kenneth Katzman, "Iran's Long-Range Missile Capabilities," Report of the Commission to Assess the Ballistic Missile Threat to the United States, July 15, 1998, Pursuant to Public Law 201, 104th Congress, Appendix III, Unclassified Working Papers, pp. 198-199; David Fillipov, "What U.S. Calls Arms Proliferation, Russia Firm Calls Business as Usual," *Boston Globe*, August 19, 1998, p. 1.

103. Moscow, *Komsomolskaya Pravda*, in Russian, October 22, 1997, *FBIS TAC*, pp. 97-295, October 23, 1997.

104. Katzman, pp. 197-202.

105. Moscow, *Radiostantsiya Ekho Moskvy*, in Russian, May 11, 1998, *FBIS SOV*, May 13, 1998, Moscow, *ITAR-TASS World Service,* in Russian, March 16, 1998, *Foreign Broadcast Information Service, Military Affairs (FBIS UMA)*, pp. 98-075, March 17, 1998, *FBIS TAC*, 98-076, March 17, 1998; see also Fred Wehling, "Russian Nuclear

and Missile Exports to Iran," *The Nonproliferation Review*, Vol. VI, No. 2, Winter, 1999, pp. 134-143.

106. Moscow, *Izvestiya* in Russian, July 18, 2000, *FBIS SOV*, July 18, 2000.

107. "No final decision to quit INF treaty - FM Lavrov," *RIA Novosti*, February 16, 2007; "Russia Made a Mistake by Scrapping Its Mid-Range Missiles-Ivanov," Moscow, Russia, *Interfax*, in English, February 7, 2007, *FBIS SOV*, February 7, 2007.

108. Moscow, *ITAR-TASS* in English, February 26, 2007, *FBIS SOV*, February 26, 2007.

109. *Ibid.*

110. *Ibid.*

111. *Ibid.*

112. Moscow, Russia, *Interfax*, in English, March 1, 2007, *FBIS SOV*, March 1, 2007.

113. Tehran, Iran, *Fars News Agency Internet Version*, in Persian, November 27, 2007, *FBIS SOV*, November 27, 2007; Paul Reynolds, "Iran's Slow But Sure Missile Advance," *BBC News*, February 3, 2009, available from *www.news.bbc.co.uk/2/hi/middle_east/7866742.htm*.

114. Moscow, *Interfax*, in Russian July 24, 2008, *FBIS SOV*, July 24, 2008.

115. Mark A. Smith, "A Russian Chronology July-September 2008," Defence Academy of the United Kingdom Advanced Research Assessment Group,, pp. 54-55, available from *www.defac.ac.uk/arag*.

116. Moscow, Russia, *Interfax* in English, August 19, 2008, *FBIS SOV*, August 19, 2008; see also "Iran Tests Rocket for Transporting Satellite, *Global Security Network*, August 18, 2008, available from *www.nti.org/d/newswire/issues/2008818.html*.

117. Reynolds.

118. Moscow, Russia, *Interfax*, in English, February 5, 2009, *FBIS SOV*, February 5, 2009.

119. Moscow, Russia, *ITAR-TASS,* in English, February 6, 2009, *FBIS SOV*, February 6, 2009.

120. *Ibid.*

121. Jacquelyn K. Davis and Robert L. Pfaltzgraff JR., *Iran With Nuclear Weapons: Anticipating the Consequences for U.S. Policy,* Washington, DC: Institute For Foreign Policy Analysis, 2008, p. 41.

122. Dennis M. Gormley, *Missile Contagion: Cruise Missile Pro-liferation and the Threat to International Security,* Westport, CT, and Washington, DC: Praeger Security International, 2008.

123. Greg Miller, "U.S. Now Sees Iran as Pursuing Nuclear Bomb," *Los Angeles Times*, February 12, 2009, available from *www.latimes.com*.

124. Tehran, Iran, *Jomhuri-ye Eslami Internet Version*, in Per-sian, September 11, 2007, "U.S. May Station Ballistic Missiles In-stead of Interceptors in Poland," Moscow, Russia, September 11, 2007, *FBIS SOV*, September 11, 2007.

125. Vladimir Rukavishnikov, "The U.S.-Russian Dispute Over Missile Defense," *Connections: The Quarterly Journal*, Fall, 2008, p. 85n.

126. *Ibid.*, p. 801.

127. "Special TV Programme "A Conversation with Vladimir Putin Continued," December 3, 2009, available from *www.premier.gov.ru/eng/events/4255.html*.

128. Ellen Barry, "Putin sounds Warning on Arms Talks," *New York Times*, December 30, 2009, p. A6.

129. Moscow, *IA Regnum* in Russian, December 19, 2009, *FBIS SOV*, December 29, 2009; "Ask the Expert: Putin's Missile Statement Shows 'Who's in Charge In Russia'," *Radio Free Europe Radio Liberty*, December 29, 2009, available from *www.rferl.org*.

130. CEP 20091229950191, Moscow, *Ekho Moskvy News Agency*, in Russian, 1334 GMT December 29, 2009, *FBIS SOV*, December 29, 2009; CEP 1229950264, Moscow, *Ekho Moskvy News Agency*, in Russian, 1500 GMT December 29, 2009, *FBIS SOV*, December 29, 2009, Alexander Golts, "Is Putin Wrecking Talks?" Moscow, *Yezhenedevnyi Zhurnal*, in Russian, December 30, 2009, *FBIS SOV*, January 4, 2010.

131. Andrew C. Kuchins and Thomas M. Sanderson, *The Northern Distribution Network and Afghanistan Geopolitical Challenges and Opportunities*, Washington, DC: Center for Strategic and International Studies, 2010.

132. Mikhail Zygar, "Russia's Double Standard," Moscow, *Russky Newsweek Online*, in Russian, December 20, 2009, *FBIS SOV*, December 28, 2009.

133. Moscow, *Argumenty Nedeli Online*, in Russian, November 26, 2006, *FBIS SOV*, November 26, 2009.

134. Mikhail Tsypkin, "The Challenge of Understanding the Russian Navy," Blank and Weitz, eds., *The Russian Military Today and Tomorrow*.

135. Moscow, *Kommersant.com*, in English," August 4, 2008, "Igor Sechin Tested a New Approach to Cuba," *FBIS SOV*, August 4, 2008; Moscow, *Interfax*, in Russian, August 4, 2008, *FBIS SOV*, August 4, 2008; Yevgeny Trifonov, "Friendship Out of Spite," Moscow, *Gazeta.ru*, in English, *FBIS SOV*, August 7, 2008; Roman Dobrokhotov, "No Ships to Call in Havana: Cuba Refuses Russian Military Aid," Moscow, *Novye Izvestiya*, in Russian, August 8, 2008, *FBIS SOV*, 2008; Open Source Committee, *OSC Analysis*, "Sechin Trip to Cuba, Putin Statements Boost Rumors of Russian Base," August 13, 2008, *FBIS SOV*, August 13, 2008.

136. Havana, *Gramma Internet Version*, in Spanish, July 24, 2008, *FBIS SOV*, July 24, 2008; Moscow, *Interfax-AVN Online*, in English, November 11, 2008, *FBIS SOV*, November 11, 2008.

137. *Open Source Center, Open Source Committee, OSC Analysis,* "Hard-Liner Sechin Spearheads Aggressive Russian Foreign Policy," *FBIS SOV*, September 24, 2008.

138. *Ibid.*

139. Andrei Kislyakov, "Russia, Cuba to Implement Joint Space Programs," September 23, 2008, available from *www.space-daily.com.*

140. "Russia and Venezuela Link Arms, *Jane's Intelligence Digest, May* 5, 2009, available from *www.4janes.com/subscribe/jid/doc.*

141. *FBIS SOV*, November 26, 2009.

142. Vladimir Socor, "Moscow Makes Furious But Empty Threats to Georgia and Ukraine," *Eurasia Daily Monitor*, April 14, 2008; "Ugroza Kremlya" ("The Kremlin's Threat"), April 7, 2008, *Radio Free Europe Radio Liberty Newsline*, April 8, 2008, available from *www.kommersant.com*; "Putin Hints At Splitting Up Ukraine, " *Moscow Times*, April 8, 2008; "Putin Threatens Unity of Ukraine, Georgia," *Unian*, April 7, 2008, available from *www.unian.net.*

143. "Ugroza Kremlya."

144. Available from *www.kremlin.ru/eng/sdocs/news.shtml*, August 11, 2009.

145. "Interview given by Dmitry Medvedev to Television Channel One, Russia, NTV, "August 31, 2008, available from *www.kremlin.ru/eng/speeches/2008/08/31/1850_type82916_206003.shtml.*

146. Alla Barakhova, Irina Granik, Maxim Ivanov, "Supreme Commander in Chief Wants to be Instantaneous. Dmitry Medvedev Asks to be Allowed to Use Army Without Wasting Time on Approval By Federation Council," Moscow, *Kommersant Online,* in Russian December 9, 2009, *FBIS SOV,* December 9, 2009.

147. Yuri E. Fedorov, *Medvedev's Amendments to the Law on Defence: The Consequences for Europe*, Finnish Institute of International Affairs, Briefing Paper No. 47, November 2009, p. 5.

148. *Ibid.*, p. 6.

149. *Ibid.*

150. European Security Treaty," November 29, 2009, available from *eng.kremlin.ru/text/docs/2009/11/223072.shtml.*

151. Fedorov, p. 6.

152. "Medvedev's Push for Control of Russian Military Unsettles Caucasus," *Deutsche Welle*, December 11, 2009, available from *http://www.dw-world.de/dw/article/0,,5004308,00.html?maca=en-rss-en-all-1573-rdf.*

153. Pavel Felgenhauer, "Military-Constitutional Coup," Moscow, *Novaya Gazeta Online*, in Russian, December 11, 2009, *FBIS SOV*, December 11, 2009.

154. Fedorov, p. 7.

155. Blank, "'No Need to Threaten Us, We Are Frightened of Ourselves,' Russia's Blueprint for a Police State, The New Security Strategy," pp. 19-150; Helen Belopolsky *Russia and the Challengers: Russian Alignment with China, Iran, and Iraq in the Unipolar Era*, Houndsmills, Basingstoke, UK: Palgrave Macmillan, 2009.

156. Julian Cooper, "The Funding of the Power Agencies of the Russian State, "*Power Institutions in Post-Soviet Societies*, No. 6-7, 2007, available from *www.pipss.org.*

157. Artem Simonov, "MVD: Modernization or Liquidation," Moscow, *Sobesednik Online*, in Russian November 26, 2009, *FBIS SOV*, November 27, 2009.

158. "Russia: The Latest Moves in the Clan Wars," December 4, 2009, available from *www.stratfor.com*; Alexander Golts, "The Most Important Thing Is Not to Stop," Moscow, *Yezhenedevnyi Zhurnal*, in Russian, November 27, 2009, *FBIS SOV*, November 27, 2009.

159. Barany.

160. *Ibid.*, p. 177; Gomart, pp. 87-88.

161. Nicole Ball, "Reforming Security Sector Governance," *Conflict, Security, and Development*, Vol. IV, No. 3, December, 2004, pp. 509-527.

162. Henning Schroeder, "Russia's National Security Strategy to 2020," *Russian Analytical Digests*, No 62, June 18, 2009, p. 9t.

163. Barany, pp. 162-168.

CHAPTER 2

RUSSIAN CIVIL-MILITARY RELATIONS: IS THERE SOMETHING NEW WITH MEDVEDEV?

Thomas Gomart

Civil-Military Relations (CMR) are never fixed forever. The balance between civil power and military power has been at the core of political relations since antiquity. How to guard the guards? In any country, this balance is in a perpetual state of flux. That means there are constant struggles, tensions, or adjustments between both powers, given their close proximity and their essentially different natures. This also means that CMR are one of the best vantage points to observe the leadership of any state with military forces.

In this regard, Russia is not unique. However, it certainly has particular traits that should be taken into consideration when analyzing these relations. First, Russia has a long tradition as a great power. CMR are deeply rooted in Russian strategic culture, which mixes imperial, Soviet, and post-Soviet legacies. Second, in the global nuclear balance, Russia is a power comparable only to the United States in terms of its capabilities. Third, Russia holds a permanent seat on the United Nations Security Council (UNSC). Fourth, Russia intends to rebrand itself as one of the BRIC countries (Brazil, Russia, India, China), as a geoeconomic player able to impact the global balance of power.

Given the deep-rooted tradition of the personalization of power in Russia and the consistently sensitive relationship between the Kremlin and the security community (armed forces and security services) in charge of protecting the country from both internal and external threats, CMR are a key element of the presidential leadership. In this field, Vladimir Putin's legacy after his two terms as president (2000-04 and 2004-08) is far from being insignificant. It is worth underlining three traits.[1] First, in comparison with Boris Yeltsin, Putin was seen by the security community as a professional and the *primus inter pares*. Putin very carefully established a new institutional balance within the security community with the effective involvement of the presidential leadership. Second, CMR accurately reflected Putin's personal power, both in terms of its ambitions and its limitations. It is never easy to implement a reform — *a fortiori* for the military due to its *esprit de corps*. Added to this, Putin's terms were very often described as a period of dominance for the so-called *Siloviki*, a strange mix of people coming from the security services and the armed forces. This ruling group is certainly more of a media construction than a homogeneous group of servants loyal to Putin or "Putinism." Third, Russia's great power status on the international scene is fundamental to the identity of the Russian elite. Moscow continues to promote a foreign and a security policy based on the rationale of *Derzhavnichestvo* (great power status). In other words, Russia is either a great power, or it is nothing.

In this context, since his election in March 2008, Dmitry Medvedev has faced the dramatic challenge of positioning himself vis-à-vis the armed forces, the security services, and his Prime Minister. In August 2008, the war in Georgia was his first high intensity crisis. This war clearly marked a turning point for the new Russian leadership, and reminds commentators that analysing CMR in Russia is not always a purely academic pastime. At first glance, Medvedev's own position in CMR is quite uncomfortable. It is one thing to deal with Putin's legacy on CMR—in itself very challenging for a young president unfamiliar with the security community, its codes, and its practices/habits—it is another to do so with Putin as Prime Minister. However, reform within the Russian security community is ongoing, and its implementation has proceeded apace in the course of 2009. This reform has been largely unremarked upon by Western policymakers. Given Putin's legacy and his current position, as well as attempts to reform the military, two basic issues deserve to be raised.

First of all, who is the *primus inter pares*? This is not simply an institutional question, it is a question of perception, and consequently of leadership. As any journalist would remind us, the Russian eagle has two heads. Consequently, we should ask: is there a coordinated, effective action coming from the current duumvirate, supported by Minister of Defense Anatoly Serdyukov, to consistently implement military reform? To what extent is this political effort successful? In this view, Lajos Szaszdi presents an interesting hypothesis which deserves exploration, even if it is quite impossible to assess it precisely. Szaszdi identifies a heavy presence of the Russian Federal Security Service (FSB) within the Russian military, which became visible in 1996 and was accelerated after 1999. This penetration can contribute to explain the efficient implementation of the reform within the armed forces.[2]

Secondly, in a more prospective view, is there a possible evolution of Russian CMR model towards a "pattern of political military partnership"? This notion has been developed by Yoram Peri to describe the Israel Defense Forces (IDF) before the war in Lebanon

(2006) and the operations in Gaza (December 2008). This concept is based on the assumption that armed and security forces have become heavyweight players in the running of state affairs and exert strong influence on international affairs. According to Peri, "the model of political-military partnership that developed in Israel at the end of the 20th century might well anticipate similar civil-military relations in democracies throughout the 21st century."[3] While remembering that Israeli CMR are specific, given the fact that Israel has been at war since its creation, it is worth utilizing this model to compare Russian CMR with Israeli ones, much more than with those models seen in most Western democratic countries. Indeed, it is worth noting that every Russian president has been faced with war: Yeltsin in Chechnya (1994-96), Putin in Chechnya (1999-2008), and Medvedev in Georgia (2008). There is no doubt that warfare is constitutive of Russian political leadership.

With these two questions in mind, our current understanding of Russian CMR should focus not only on the functioning of the duumvirate, but also base itself on observations inside and outside the security community. Comparison is required with external models but also with Russian/Soviet historical patterns. In this area, we are witnessing a period of methodological convergence, which could be exploited politically. One the one hand, Western expertise has understood that it makes no sense to strictly apply its own models of democratic civilian control, as they were exported to Central and Eastern Europe during the so-called "transition," to the complex realities of Russian experiences. Russian traditions of militarism continue to shape the mind-set of the Russian security elites. On the other hand, the Russian top brass has clearly assimilated many concepts and ideas coming from the West (and from other countries such as Israel) about CMR. Recent publications tend to illustrate that the Russian military no longer holds a self-referential vision for the Russian security establishment.[4] These two trends may offer more opportunities to address CMR issues when dealing with Russia.

In a July 2009 article, Dale Herspring explains how military culture is crucial to understand and practice CMR in polities such as Russia and the United States.[5] Looking at two periods in both countries (Yeltsin and George Bush I, and Putin and George Bush II), Herspring argues that there were strong deficiencies in terms of understanding military culture. This chapter will not discuss Herspring's convincing argument, but makes use of the three key factors identified by Herspring: executive leadership, respect for military expertise, and the chain of command. These three components are crucial to the establishment of a "political-military partnership" as suggested by Peri. I intend to use this framework to analyze the Russian duumvirate, to identify recent evolutions, and to speculate that military culture as described by Herspring is the indispensable glue for a partnership, which may be under construction in Russia right now.

EXECUTIVE LEADERSHIP

Advantages of the Duumvirate.

Because of his background as FSB Director and Secretary General of the Security Council (and lastly as Prime Minister), Putin was well-versed in security matters when he was appointed, and soon after elected, president. He manifested his personal interest in security issues, which certainly, at that time shaped, his vision of the world, and were the main determinant in his distribution of power. There is no doubt that the Kremlin's supremacy in decisionmaking on security policy was reinforced under Putin.[6] Nor is there any doubt that foreign policy is subordinated to security policy in the Russian case. In contrast to the Yeltsin period, Putin's Russia regained real freedom of action on the international stage.[7] This comeback could be explained in different ways, but one of them is the rebuilding of offensive military capabilities.[8]

In comparison, Medvedev appears to have been very green in the security business. His lack of experience was seen as one of his most visible weaknesses when he was competing with Sergey Ivanov to become Putin's successor. In retrospect, this apparent weakness seems to have been converted into a competitive advantage. His political basis was established through his administrative capabilities, his links with *Gazprom*, and his ability to promote so-called "national projects." Thanks to them, in the media he appeared more socially-oriented than security-oriented. Added to this, Putin was sure not to welcome competition in his master field. Due to their differences of origins and style, this duumvirate covers a larger political spectrum than an association between Putin and Ivanov would.

Under Medvedev, there has also been a change in the legal possibilities for military force; by removing constitutional constraints on military intervention abroad in November 2009, Medvedev has widened the executive leadership's options. Medvedev signed a law allowing the president to decide on his own the operational use of the Russian armed forces abroad, as well as the number of troops deployed (Previously, as written in the 1993 Constitution, the Federation Council's approval was required before allowing or disallowing use of force.).

Another very important point is that the cabinet, headed by the Prime Minister, carries responsibilities for Russian external relations. Unlike his predecessors as prime minister, Putin clearly maintains a heavy hand in security policy.[9] Given his experience as president, Putin understands perfectly well the impact of this security policy on Russian foreign policy, and the need to promote them to both the Russian public and Russia's foreign partners. It is the first time since 1991 that Russia has had such a powerful Prime Minister, who is acting more as a highly influential Vice-President rather than as the boss of ministers. This leads to the conclusion that, acting together, this duumvirate can exert strong pressure on the Russian security establishment given its internal popularity and its external contacts.

Dealing with War.

As has already been noted, since the collapse of the Union of Soviet Socialist Republics (USSR), the Russian leadership, from Yeltsin to Medvedev, has had to deal with armed conflict. War is closely linked to leadership in Russia. To some extent, it can be said that every Russian leader should be tested at war before being fully recognized as a full-scale president. War seems to be an implicit step in the *cursus honorum*.

The second war in Chechnya is crucial to understand Putin's accession to the presidency in 2000. In fact, he demonstrated his appetite for military leadership when he was still Prime Minister. The decline of Yeltsin's political influence combined with the military's desire for revenge and the divisions at the top of the security community gave Putin some room to show his resolution.[10] In fact, when Putin acceded to power, he exploited the political vacuum left by Yeltsin in the security field. Yeltsin "was not interested in armed forces," and created an incomplete presidential leadership that affected the High Command.[11] Putin never considered Chechnya to be an ethnic conflict, but rather a conflict between civilization and barbarians. From the start, he made no distinction between terrorists and separatists, using the "international terrorism" concept as a way to establish his leadership internally and to brand his image externally. On this very last point, Chechnya was a field for various critics coming from abroad (mainly from Europe) but also a field to promote himself as a tough leader (terrorists should be "shot in the outhouses"). On the conduct of operations, he was very careful in dealing with the "Chechen generals," taking time to insist on the need for cooperation between the armed forces and the security forces. In short, Chechnya has been the main tool used by Putin to implement his leadership internally.

The problem with Georgia is different, given the fact that this war was conducted outside the Russian Federation. From this point of view, Georgia is a very telling case study for the implementation of leadership externally. It is too early to know if Medvedev would have preferred to do so only diplomatically. However, it is worth remembering that he took his first main initiative in foreign policy in May 2008 by promoting his 'initiative' for a new pan-European security architecture. Three months later, Russia was at war with Georgia, and Moscow severely damaged its relations with the North Atlantic Treaty Organization

(NATO) and the European Union (EU). The "disproportionate use of force" figured among the numerous
criticisms of Russian behavior by Western officials in
the aftermath of the war. On September 1, 2008, the
EU condemned Russia for this reason. Many Russian
officials seemed unable to understand this condemna-
tion conceptually.[12] This lack of understanding can
be explained by the differences in the language of
leadership between both sides. In the West, generally
speaking, the concept of leadership is mainly seen as
the judicious use of management tools. In the business sphere, leadership is the means to make an organization or group to move in a chosen direction. John
Keegan points out that "modern economists preach
moderation." Indeed, self-control and moderation are
very often presented as key factors of success in the
management literature. In Russia, generally speaking,
the concept of leadership remains security-oriented.
The important point to highlight is that, as Keegan
reminds us: "there is no place . . . for moderation in
warfare."[13] In Russian strategic culture, the only concern is final victory, an end which is justified, even if
it can only be won by means of extreme ruthlessness.
Therefore, Russian officials believe that Russian forces
calibrated the use of force in Georgia pretty well: "another option would have been to use the same methods as NATO in Serbia."[14]

From this point of view, the real challenge for the
executive leadership is more internal than external: it
is to offer the military the proper political conditions
and framework to use force in pursuit of the state's
objectives. Seen from outside, some decisions may ap-
pear irrational when, in fact, they are quite rational
in the Russian context, owing to the particular inter-
face between the political and military leaderships.[15]

In Chechnya, Putin gave the security community opportunities to operate with a free hand, as if his background makes him tolerant to violence. In addition, Putin is convinced of the need to use force to be respected internationally. For the Russian leadership, international respect chimes with fear. It is too early to know whether Medvedev was a moderating factor in Georgia. However, in terms of executive leadership, there was apparently a division of labor between the Prime Minister and the President. The latter was mainly involved in the diplomatic phase of the conflict, moving away from military confrontation by negotiating the ceasefire. It can be said that the executive leadership based on the duumvirate was efficient and successful in conducting the military operations and attaining its political objectives. It was also lucky. In fact the degree of success is relative. The Russian military success was mainly due to the Russian armed forces' numerical superiority.[16] In this way, the military leadership succeeded in compensating for its inferior equipment and training failures by managing its numerical advantage. In the diplomatic field, the success is much more debatable, given the fact that the recognition of South Ossetia and Abkhazia isolated the Russian Federation on the international scene, and will inhibit its capacity for initiative in foreign policy for many years.

Crisis Management.

The sinking of the *Kursk* in August 2000 was the lowest point of the Russian military's decline, it was also the first real test for Putin. In terms of domestic crisis management, it was a complete disaster. The accident revealed the troubled state of CMR 1 year after Putin took over from Yeltsin and gave an insight into Putin's style of leadership when dealing with the military.[17] On this occasion, Putin realized the duplicity of the high command and became determined to reinforce his control over it. He did so, however, very carefully, avoiding direct confrontation with the military. The sinking revealed the reluctance of the top brass to deal openly with an accident and to accept foreign help. Interestingly, this event was not at all used against the military, particularly not the navy. Given his political weakness at that time, the young president avoided tackling the High Command head on (despite many reasons to do so), but attributed the disaster to the very poor state of the armed forces. Consequently, the *Kursk* led to the decision to increase the military budget significantly, even when the Russian economy was still very weak. In retrospect, the sinking of the *Kursk* offers a case study of executive leadership amid adverse conditions. The circumstances of the sinking and failed rescue operation are not significant; the point is that Putin gave political meaning to the accident in order to tighten his grasp on the military.

The second crisis managed by Putin was the Beslan hostage taking in September 2004. It is the main turning point in Putin's double term, prompting both external and internal changes. The event was in itself a trauma for the both the leadership and the public. It has certainly been underestimated by the Western expertise, given the fact that it occurred in a context where the Russian security policy was already becoming more assertive. However, this event profoundly affected Russian domestic policy (it was used to justify administrative restructuring, probably decided upon before the crisis) as well as security policy.[18] According to

Putin, "international terrorism," to which Russia had been subjected, should be eradicated by all means and firstly by the reinforcement of the state. It was also used as the main conceptual tool to force the security community, and firstly the armed forces, to reconsider their priorities, organization, and doctrine. In fact, Putin used Beslan to change the hierarchy of threats. He explicitly disassociated Beslan from Chechnya by presenting the hostage taking as an attack of "international terrorism" and claiming that Russia was facing a "total, cruel, war on a large scale." It is significant to note the conflation of a classical understanding of interstate power relations and a transnational reading of mass terrorism. Putin used this crisis to redesign the threat perception system. It was crucial to do so in order to justify the military reform.

At present, Medvedev has not yet had to deal with a crisis involving CMR. It is, for instance, too early to draw political conclusions from the bombing of the Nevsky Express in November 2009. However, in terms of executive leadership Medvedev seems to be in line with Putin, underlining transnational threats to justify and impose military reform.

RESPECT FOR MILITARY EXPERTISE

Use of Force and Utility of Force.

Apparently, Rupert Smith was not read only in the West:[19] The Russian leadership is quite well acquainted with the paradigm of war among the people. According to Herspring,[20] Putin, when he was Prime Minister, "made it clear to the generals that he was interested in their ideas on the use of force." Even if it was politically risky, Putin approved plans prepared by his high command, especially in the North Caucasus. In his thinking, there is a strong link between military objectives and political achievements in order to reestablish federal authority. However, this personal interest for the use of force led to strong debates regarding the North Caucasus between the armed forces, the FSB, and the Ministry of Internal Affairs (MVD) about the means to adopt. There were not only debates on the nature of the Chechen war itself, but also a more technical approach on the best tools to be used to fight terrorists among a civilian population.[21] In Putin's understanding of the use of force, there is also his personal experience from Kosovo. When NATO hit Serbia in 1999, he was head of the FSB. Externally, Kosovo convinced him of the necessity of reconsidering Russia's security policy.[22] Internally, at that time the Russian army's reputation was suffering from its poor performance in Chechnya. For the Russian top brass, the crisis in the Balkans offered "an opportunity for redemption."[23] In June 1999, the decision by the military to take Pristina airport with 200 paratroopers revealed the dysfunctional CMR and the high tensions between the Russian Ministry of Foreign Affairs (MFA) and the Ministry of Defense (MoD). From Putin's point of view, this event and these tensions were very damaging for Russia's credibility as a player in the Balkans. The future president learned an important lesson: The military did not hesitate to take the initiative irrespective of the country's official diplomatic position. In other words, the respect for military expertise should be complemented with the military's respect for and obedience to the president.

As president, Medvedev also allowed the military to use force in Georgia. Even if there were some operational deficiencies, the Russian forces achieved victory.[24] This was particularly significant to the Russian leadership as a whole, given that the Georgian army was receiving American and Israeli aid. More important, Russia can proclaim a military victory in Caucasus after many years of frustration in Chechnya. This intervention in the Georgian land provoked public debates in Russia over the use of force, and consequently the possible role of the military as an instrument of Russian foreign policy. This debate is not only about political and constitutional constraints on military intervention abroad, but also about the possibility of increasingly frequent use of force in international relations in the future, as seen by the Russian leadership.[25] From this point of view, there is clearly a link between these debates and the notion of "sphere of special interests" promoted by Medvedev.[26] Regarding the current president's respect for military expertise, the situation has changed in the aftermath of the war. Indeed, celebrating victory and achievement of the operational goals set by the Kremlin has not dispelled "an atmosphere of uncertainty concerning the future of Russia's conventional forces."[27] Not an expert on security matters himself, Medvedev immediately used this victory to pressure the High Commend to focus on the modernization of the armed forces, in terms of equipment and personnel structures.

Two Interconnected Tools: Reform and Budget.

After his election, Putin started to push the military to become a professional force. It was a risky task as the High Command was very reluctant to professionalize. The reform promoted by Putin and mainly implemented by Ivanov targeted several objectives. First, the design of the military forces needed to be redefined so as to create compact and mobile forces that were able to be deployed abroad. This wish was due to different threat analysis, which highlighted requirements other than the traditional risk of interstate confrontation. Second, the reform was a means to reduce the social power of the conscription-based military. The conditions for personnel within the ranks is certainly one of the most sensitive issues for Russian public opinion. Last, but not least, the reform was a way for the "civilian" leadership (both Putin and Ivanov) to gradually dominate the High Command. Ultimately, Putin and Ivanov were clearly determined to lead a reform extending beyond the dismissal of the most emblematic figure of the military institution. Both men marked "their joint will to rebalance the civil and military spheres to the benefit of civilian leadership with close ties to the security services."[28]

In retrospect, it is interesting to analyze the parallel careers of Ivanov and Medvedev, who were competitors, especially during Putin's second term. Military reform was Ivanov's main political instrument for self-promotion. He was successful in consolidating his influence as deputy prime minister (November 2005), and afterwards as first deputy prime minister (February 2007). Given these promotions and a background similar to that of Putin (which, in fact, may have been a disadvantage), there were high expectations that Ivanov would succeed Putin. However, Ivanov's achievements were seen as less significant than Medvedev's success in other areas through the so-called "national projects."

However, three key successes can be attributed to Ivanov: (1) the dismissal of General Anatoli Kvashnin, (2) the reestablishment of the Ministry of Defense at the top of the military chain of command, and (3) his own succession by a real civilian minister.[29] There is a clear continuation between Putin and Medvedev: the use of reform as a political tool to make the military change. Putin started the process with a disaster (*Kursk*) while Medvedev has continued with a military success (Georgia). It is certainly easier to put pressure on the top brass after having satisfied its thirst for prestige. On September 2008, Medvedev gave five priorities: (1) permanent readiness for troops, (2) efficiency of the command system, (3) improvement of training, (4) new weapons, and (5) social conditions. This very ambitious reform was announced in the aftermath of the war before the Russian economy really began suffering from the worldwide financial crisis. The situation completely changed 18 months later in that Russia was in deep recession in 2009 (gross domestic product [GDP] fell 8.5 percent). In this context, the good news is that Medvedev, Putin, and Serdyukov are acting in the same direction by using the topic of reform to dominate the military; the bad news is that the financial constraints are tight, and limit the potential for deep reform.

Born in 1962, Serdyukov seems to have a talent for discretion as well as efficient reform within the armed forces.[30] He has no military experience except his time as a conscript. His reform effort is supported by both sides of the duumvirate, and Serdyukov has first of all increased his control on the budget to make the top brass change. In April 2009, Liubov Kudelina, Deputy Defense Minister in charge of finances, left the Ministry of Defense (MoD); she was originally appointed by Sergei Ivanov. In June 2008, following a dispute over proposed cuts to the officer corps, Serdyukov evicted Alexandr Rukshin, former chief of the MoD's Main Operations Directorate. The same month, the head of the General Staff General Yuri Baluyevsky left his position. Serdykov's attempts to extend military purchases beyond Russian industry provoked strong reactions not only from the national monopolies, but also from the Parliament.[31]

Serdyukov's actions to increase control over the military budget have generated consistent complaints from the top brass and from the defense industry. He is very often presented as an inexperienced civilian minister, unable to deal with operational challenges.[32] However, Serdykov persevered on the path of reform, and announced a radical break in October 2008 just after the war in Georgia. The General Staff and its autonomy were clearly targeted for reduction, with 13,500 of its 22,000 positions slated for elimination.[33] The General Staff is in charge of strategic planning. Regaining political responsibility for this task is one crucial justification for the reform and the redesign of the armed forces. Since the departure of Baluyevsky, the General Staff has been run by General Nikolai Makarov, whose prominent task in the reform process has seemed to deflect criticism from his immediate civilian boss.

CLEAR CHAIN OF COMMAND

At the Top Level.

Having observed the very negative consequences of an unclear chain of command under Yeltsin, given the constant bickering between Igor Sergeyev and Anatoly Kvashnin, Putin gradually used his authority to silence their disputes. The fight between the MoD and the General Staff not only damaged the image of the military establishment, but also damaged the operational efficiency of the chain of command. It was one of the most obvious conclusions of the first war in Chechnya. At the beginning of the second war in Chechnya, Putin gave his generals a free hand in conducting operations at the expense of the Ministry of Internal Affairs (MVD). However, Putin's initial trust in his generals progressively changed given their tendency to openly ignore the political leadership when fixing military objectives. In 2004, the dismissal of General Kvashnin shifted the gravitational center of the presidential administration/General Staff/MoD to the benefit of the ministry. This led Putin to reinforce the FBS's responsibilities, not only in Chechnya.

The gradual concentration of power around the presidency under Putin gave him much more influence in strategic decisionmaking and planning. Putin and his team supervised the designation of political objectives and discussion with the High Command of related military objectives. Under Putin, Chechnya was at the core of politico-military relations, and clearly the level of coordination between politico-military interfaces improved significantly. This was due to Putin's personal leadership and the use of the threat of international terrorism to justify new approaches and new forms of organization.

In fact, the key issue remains threat perception at the highest level and its translation into strategic planning. As already discussed, Medvedev used the war in Georgia as the main tool for pursuing reform. He is convinced that this reform can be best accomplished within the context of a successful military campaign. In terms of threat perception, Medvedev now has to combine a set of complex processes: evolutions in the relationship with the United States (including Ballistic Missile Defense (BMD), the new NATO Strategic

Concept, Afghanistan, and Iran), evolutions in the relationship with China, experience drawn from the war in Georgia, the continuing instability in North Caucasus, and terrorist operations such as the *Nevsky Express* bombing.

Small wars are always present, big war is still always possible: here is the discourse promoted to maintain the system and to justify the current power organization based on a large security community able to exert a strong social influence on society and to project it on the political leadership. This dual-track influence is fuelled by an old-fashioned conscription system related to an old-fashioned threat perception system. The latter has fixed the Russian homeland as encircled by adversaries, namely Western countries. At the end of Putin's first term, it was often estimated that the Russian military threats were formulated mainly by the military intelligence Russian Special Forces (GRU) in the framework of the High Command.[34] The political decline of the High Command and the changes in the organization of the GRU may have changed these habits. However and whatever the recent evolutions are, it is worth noting that in its political communication "the regime has waged 10 different 'wars'" over the last 5 years.[35] In other words, war is a discourse used by the Russian leadership well beyond military affairs. Such a discourse echoes pretty well with the traditions of militarism deeply rooted in the different levels of Russian society.

Recent decisions and statements cannot be properly understood without taking these traditions of militarism into consideration. Even if there is a political wish to reform and to modernize the armed forces, there is strong resistance from the military establishment, which is very capable, not only in Russia, of protecting its institutional interests. However, it seems that, right now, there is much more agreement between the top brass and the political leadership, simply because the latter is more powerful. Given the experience of Kvashnin and Baluyevsky, the current Chief of the General Staff, Nikolai Makarov presents himself and his institution as supportive of the reform. He denies that "opposition from the generals" continues to present a barrier to the reform of the military.[36] In the discourse at least, there is a consensus for pursuing the reform according to the direction given by the political leadership. This reform is now a must for Medvedev and Putin, given the fact they perceived the war in Georgia as a setback to their efforts of projecting the image of a resurgent Russia.[37] In other words, the success or the failure of the reform will have a direct impact on the diplomatic stance of the Russian Federation in the coming years.

New Design and Reshuffle.

Under Putin, Russia's political leadership succeeded in reestablishing itself at the top of the chain of command. This was achieved gradually, and not forever. In fact, CMR are continually in flux and largely depend on the domestic context as well as the conduct of operations. Medvedev has the benefit of Putin's legacy, even if he is constantly under pressure to demonstrate his leadership in this particular field. The reform is driven by the wish to redesign the military organization in different sectors. For instance, special attention is paid to the MoD information services, which were overhauled in October 2009: many positions are no more reserved exclusively for officers, but open to civilian experts.[38]

The armed forces are divided into three main services (army, navy, and air force) and three separate branches (strategic forces, space forces, and airborne forces). One of the main efforts for reformatting focuses on the ground forces. The four-tiered command system (military district-army-division-regiment) is supposed to be replaced with the three-tiered system (military district-army-brigade). These attempts require strong political and financial resources, given the need to close down many units and consequently to remove thousands of command positions. The aim is to make the forces more mobile in order to improve their capabilities of projection and increase the level of readiness. They have deep consequences in terms of education and training. On this last point, it is said that command should be now more focused on the individual skills of officers and troops. The main target is to improve the capabilities on the tactical level, having in mind the evolution of many European armies. In terms of command at this level, it is worth noting the opening of the new noncommissioned officer (NCO) training centre at Ryazan in December 2009. Russian ground forces are asked to significantly improve their modularity, mobility, and operational self-sufficiency.

This type of reform requires a strong political hand and an ability to mobilize key military executives, while removing reluctant ones. From this point of view, many appointments (and dismissals) related to these changes of structures have occurred recently. In terms of figures, there is apparently a wave of change. The officer corps is supposed to be reduced by 205,000 in 2016 (initially in 2012). In addition, there are very brutal changes at the highest level of the military: for instance, of the 50 top military officials, it is estimated that 44 have been replaced since February 2007.[39] For the reform and the proper balance in CMR, a key factor remains the position of the security services, which have very recently exerted a disproportionate influence in comparison with other armies.

The fight between the GRU and the KGB-FSB has been characteristic of Russian CMR for a long time. This tension between the military intelligence structure and the civilian security services (also responsible for monitoring the officer corps) is rooted in the past totalitarian power structure. Some consequences are still visible. To some extent, the recent developments of the reform process have consisted in subjecting the High Command, and consequently the GRU, which played a crucial role in the strategic planning and in the control of special forces, to the political leadership.

In April 2009, Korabelnikov, head of the GRU, was removed. In terms of command, special forces were removed from the control of the GRU and reassigned to the military districts: "It seems that the FSB is now close to victory in the long-running competition for power and influence between the civilian and military intelligence agencies."[40] This assessment deserves to be observed in the medium term, but if it is confirmed, it is certainly a key step in the reform process.

CONCLUSION

Returning to the initial question: Is there something new with Medvedev in terms of CMR? — I would answer no and yes. No, given the fact that there is a visible continuation of the reforming trend launched by Putin in imposing the political leadership's control of the military leadership. This effort achieved many concrete results. Both men are convinced by the need to transform the security community and the armed forces into a more professional, compact, and mobile instrument. Military expenditure has increased significantly over the last 10 years. It should continue to allow the procurement of new weapons (also abroad) and improve the level of training. At the same time, control of financial resources remains the political leadership's main tool to make the High Command change.

Yes, given the fact that CMR are always in flux, and need to be adapted to circumstances. Medvedev did so quite smartly. In fact, there was an apparent acceleration of the reform process after the war in Georgia. This war highlighted numerous flaws in the conduct of operations as well as the level of equipment. However, Russian forces were victorious, creating a much more comfortable framework to implement reform. In any case, threat perception remains at the core of CMR for the coming years. On this also, changes will not necessarily follow a linear path. The reform of the armed forces remains a risky challenge for the Russian leadership, and for its foreign counterparts.

ENDNOTES - CHAPTER 2

1. Thomas Gomart, *Russian Civil-Military Relations: Putin's Legacy*, Washington, DC: Carnegie Endowment for International Peace, 2008, pp. 2-3.

2. Lajos Szàszdi, *Russian Civil-Military Relations and the Origins of the Second Chechen War*, Lanham, MD: University Press of America, 2009, p. 284.

3. Yoram Peri, *Generals in the Cabinet Room*, Washington, DC: United States Institute of Peace, 2006, p. 9.

4. Major-General Sergei Pechurov, in *Krasnaya Zvezda*, September 2009, pp. 25, 26, 27. See also Jacob Kipp, "Moscow Exam-

ines an Alternative Vision of Military Professionalism ," *Eurasia Daily Monitor*, October 7, 2009, pp. 6, 184.

5. Dale Herspring, "Civil-Military Relations in the United States and Russia," *Armed Forces & Society*, Vol. 35, No. 4, July 2009, pp. 667-687.

6. Bobo Lo, *Vladimir Putin and the Evolution of Russian Foreign Policy*, London, UK: Blackwell Publishing/RIIA, 2003, pp. 42-49.

7. Thomas Gomart, "Russian Foreign Policy: Strange Inconsistency," *Russian Series* 06/12 (E), Defence Academy of the UK, CSRC, March 2006.

8. Steve Rosefielde, *Russia in the 21st Century, The Prodigal Superpower*, Cambridge, UK: Cambridge University Press, 2005.

9. Jeffrey Mankoff, *Russian Foreign Policy, The Return of Great Power Politics*, Lanham, MD: Rowman and Littlefield, 2009, p. 13.

10. Timothy Colton, *Yeltsin, A Life*, New York: Basic Books, 2008, pp. 430-431.

11. Dale Herspring, *The Kremlin and the High Command: Presidential Impact on the Russian Military from Gorbachev to Putin*, Lawrence, KS: University Press of Kansas, 2006, p. 119.

12. High-ranked Russian Official, interview with the author, Paris, France, December 2008.

13. John Keegan, *The Mask of Command*, London, UK: Pimlico, 2004, pp. 2-3.

14. High-ranked Russian Official, interview with the author, London, UK: December 2009.

15. David Capezza, "Translating Russia's Military Reform," *Small Wars Journal*, April 2009, *smallwarsjournal.com/blog/2009/04/translating-russia-military-r/*.

16. Tor Bukkvoll, "Russia's Military Performance in Georgia," *Military Review*, November-December 2009, pp. 57-62.

17. Robert Brannon, *Russian Civil-Military Relations*, Burlington, Ashgate, UK: 2009, p. 138.

18. Dov Lynch, "'The Enemy is at the Gate': Russia after Beslan," *International Affairs*, Vol. 81, No. 2, 2006, pp. 97-114.

19. Rupert Smith, *The Utility of Force*, London, UK: Penguin Books, 2006.

20. Herspring, "Civil-Military Relations in the United States and Russia," p. 676.

21. Gomart, *Russian Civil-Military Relations*, p. 78.

22. Vladimir Baranovsky, "The Kosovo Factor in Russia's Foreign Policy," *The International Spectator*, n° 2, April-June 2000, p. 113-130.

23. Brannon, *Russian Civil-Military Relations*, p. 77.

24. Roy Allison, "Russia Resurgent? Moscow's Campaign to 'Coerce Georgia to Peace'," *International Affairs*, Vol. 73, No. 5, 2008, pp. 23-33.

25. Brandon Stewart and Yuri Zhukov, "Use of force and civil-military relations in Russia: an automated content analysis," *Small Wars & Insurgencies*, Vol. 20, No. 2, June 2009, pp. 319-343.

26. On the link between the reform within the military and this notion, see Roger McDermott, "The Restructuring of the Modern Russian Army," *Journal of Slavic Military Studies*, Vol. 22, 2009, p. 501.

27. Roger McDermott, "Russia's Conventional Armed Forces and the Georgian War ," *Parameters*, Vol. XXXIX, No. 1, 2009, pp. 67-68.

28. Gomart, *Russian Civil-Military Relations* , p. 69.

29. *Ibid*.

30. "Genstab vistroil novij oblik" ("General Staff has set up a new image"), *Nezavissimaïa Gazeta*, December 30, 2009.

31. "Minister Serdioukov atakuiout po vsem frontam" ("Minister Serdioukov launches an attack on numerous fronts"), *Nezavissimaïa Gazeta*, November 23, 2009.

32. McDermott, "Russia's Conventional Armed Forces and the Georgian War," p. 69.

33. Dmitry Gorenburg, "Russia's New Model Army, The Ongoing Radical Reform of the Russian Military," PONARS Eurasia Policy Memo No. 78, September 2009.

34. Stephen Forss, "Russian Military Thinking and Threat Perception: A Finnish View," CERI Strategy Papers, n° 5, November 2009, p. 6. The author refers to research made by the Swedish Defense Research Establishment FOI (Spring 2004).

35. Andrei Illarionov, "The *Siloviki* in Charge," *Journal of Democracy*, Vol. 20, No. 2, April 2009, p. 72.

36. Roger McDermott, "The Restructuring of the Modern Russian Army," *Journal of Slavic Military Studies*, Vol. 22, 2009, p. 487.

37. McDermott, "Russia's Conventional Armed Forces and the Georgian War," p. 78.

38. Roger McDermott, "Russian Defense Ministry Reorganizes Information Services," *Eurasia Daily Monitor*, Vol. 6, issue 192, October 20, 2009.

39. "Housecleaning at the Top," October 19, 2009, available from *russiamil.wordpress.com/*.

40. "Reforming the GRU," November 17, 2009, available from *russiamil.wordpress.com/*.

U.S. ARMY WAR COLLEGE

Major General Gregg F. Martin
Commandant

*****

STRATEGIC STUDIES INSTITUTE

Director
Professor Douglas C. Lovelace, Jr.

Director of Research
Dr. Antulio J. Echevarria II

Editor
Dr. Stephen J. Blank

Director of Publications
Dr. James G. Pierce

Publications Assistant
Ms. Rita A. Rummel

*****

Composition
Mrs. Jennifer E. Nevil

www.ingramcontent.com/pod-product-compliance
Lightning Source LLC
Chambersburg PA
CBHW080207300326

41934CB00038B/3397